Understanding Plato

DAVID J. MELLING

Oxford   New York

OXFORD UNIVERSITY PRESS

Oxford University Press, Walton Street, Oxford OX2 6DP

Oxford New York Toronto
Delhi Bombay Calcutta Madras Karachi
Petaling Jaya Singapore Hong Kong Tokyo
Nairobi Dar es Salaam Cape Town
Melbourne Auckland
and associated companies in
Berlin Ibadan

Oxford is a trade mark of Oxford University Press

British Library Cataloguing in Publication Data

Melling, David J.
Understanding Plato.
1. Plato
I. Title
184   B395
ISBN 0–19–219129–2
ISBN 0–19–289116–2 Pbk

Library of Congress Cataloging in Publication Data

Melling, David J.
Understanding Plato.
(An OPUS book)
Bibliography: p.   Includes index.
1. Plato.   I. Title.   II. Series: OPUS.
B395.M35   1987   184   87–7824
ISBN 0–19–219129–2
ISBN 0–19–289116–2 (pbk.)

Printed in Great Britain by
Biddles Ltd.
Guildford and King's Lynn

Preface

This book is written as an introduction to Plato and his writings. It presents him to you not as the creator of a complete unchanging philosophical system, but rather as what he was, a man of his own day who grappled with an agenda of problems and issues generated initially by the arguments of his predecessors and contemporaries, a man with the determination to wrestle with difficult philosophical problems throughout his life into extreme old age without ever losing that flexibility and vitality of mind which enabled him to reconsider, change, modify, and sometimes abandon the conclusions he came to at various stages in his life. It does not attempt to present an analysis of all Plato's works, still less of all his arguments. Some dialogues, even important ones, are scarcely mentioned. The book is not a complete map of Plato's thought and writings; it is more of a route-guide, leading you through Plato's philosophical work, pointing to what the author believes to be the most significant and important features of his thoughtscape, and suggesting interesting detours into surrounding territory that you may care to explore for yourself at leisure.

This book presents one man's view of Plato and his work; it makes no pretence to offer an objective and balanced appraisal of the long and rich tradition of Platonic scholarship, or even of its contemporary state. The account of Plato presented here owes much to the work of others, but the synthesis remains personal.

I wish to acknowledge the great debt I owe to my teachers, especially Professor Dorothy Emmett and Professor Czeslaw Lejewski whose lectures on Plato stirred an enthusiasm for him I have never lost; to my colleagues, especially Wolfe Mays, Stewart Linney, Harry Lesser, Mike Garfield, Peter Caldwell, and Lawrence Moonan, and to OUP's reader for helpful discussion and criticism; to my students at Bolton Institute of Higher Education, at Manchester Polytechnic, and at Manchester University for many helpful questions, arguments, and speculations;

to Sheila Hill, Tina Menges, and Sue Thorne for the generous help they have given in the preparation of the manuscript; to Harpal Bahra for encouragement; and to my editors at Oxford University Press for their patience and help.

D. J. M.

Contents

Note on sources

Throughout this book, where specific passages from Plato's text are quoted, you will find a page number and letter given. These are the 'Stephanus' numbers which refer to the pages and sections of the standard edition of Plato's text and will usually be found in the margins of all translations. The actual translations contained in this volume are, unless otherwise acknowledged, my own.

1
Plato's life and background

Plato was born about 427 BCE into an aristocratic Athenian family, a wealthy household living at what had been for some four centuries the cultural hub of the Greek world. His parents' and grandparents' generations had lived through the half-century during which Athens rose to her greatest power and magnificence, and Plato's family were deeply involved in the political life of their city.

Plato's own writings are sufficient evidence that he had acquired an excellent education which, apart from developing his interest in political and social questions, had opened his mind to the entire landscape of contemporary intellectual life. He knew the poetical classics, the works of the great dramatists, the writings and researches of earlier philosophers, the techniques of literary analysis used by sophists and rhapsodes. Sophocles, Euripides, and Aristophanes were all writing during his formative years; Sophocles and Euripides both died in the year Plato was 21. Throughout the city buildings and sculptures proclaimed the wealth and glory of Athens, the open democratic society which had defeated the immense might of the Persian Empire, and which now saw itself as the definitive embodiment of Greek civilization's highest values.

The Athens of Pericles had drawn artists, writers, and philosophers from the whole of the Greek world. It offered them the chance of patronage or at least of winning a public in a state famous for its democratic constitution, its high cultural achievements, and its openness to new ideas. The world of the Greeks was united by the sea; as the major sea power Athens had come to be the commercial and intellectual lodestone of that world. Although the earliest Greek philosophers came without exception from the eastern and western extremities of the Greek world, the rise of Athenian sea power, the wealth and cultural vitality of the city under the rule of Pericles, and the ready-made market for new ideas soon exercised a magnetic influence on many major thinkers and drew them to Athens, which became the seminar room in which the latest ideas were talked through, explored, analysed, and evaluated: it became the market place in which new theories, new skills, and new forms of higher education were put on display and sold. The development of widespread literacy had not removed the potency and importance of the spoken word: in Assembly and law court alike, the skills of verbal combat were at least an essential defensive weapon for anyone with political ambitions and might conceivably be the key to power. Teachers of oratory and of the skills of debate had a ready-made audience, and in many cases an audience ready and able to pay a substantial price for the new skills and the new knowledge they were offered.

In the warm climate of Attica life was lived out of doors for much of the year. In Plato's day, the Athenians looked to the Assembly and the law courts, the theatre, the gymnasium and the agora for social life, for entertainment, for fine speech making, and for elegant conversation.

In Plato's youth, the sophist was a familiar figure, a professional exponent of the arts of argument giving a public display of his skills, a theorist of the nature of values or of the foundations of human society offering to a critical audience a display of formal oratory or of his lecturing style, his analytic powers and speculative abilities.

Amongst the educated young men of Plato's society the ideas of philosophers, both contemporary thinkers and the better-known philosophers of older generations, would have been familiar topics of discussion. Cratylus, for example, was well known as a follower of Heraclitus, propounding his own version of Heraclitus' notion that the things of everyday experience are in constant flux, and are therefore not possible objects of true knowledge. The theory of Parmenides that reality is one eternal unchanging sphere of being was widely known as were the paradoxes with which his pupil Zeno defended him against common sense and against the rival mathematically based system of the Pythagoreans. Pericles had given patronage to the philosopher Anaxagoras whose book on natural philosophy, as Plato himself informs us in the *Apology*, was available on public sale at a reasonable price. It may not have been top of the best-seller lists, but it clearly found buyers willing to grapple with the difficult notion that, while everything contains parts of everything, the parts of which things are composed are identical in nature with the things themselves. His claim that the ultimate cause of all things is Mind caught the imagination of many of his contemporaries. Something at least was known of the Pythagoreans, despite their religious reticence about their school's doctrines; their brief and dramatically terminated tenure of power in Croton would have called for comment and debate.

Some of the philosophical ideas that lay at hand to the educated Athenian were consonant with the kind of worldscape offered by the common sense of his day. Others, however, the flux theory of Heraclitus, the radical monism of Parmenides, and the baffling paradoxes of Zeno created what must have seemed an unbridgeable chasm between the data of sense experience and the implications of intellectual reasoning.

In the three centuries before Plato's birth, the Greek city-states had undertaken an enormous programme of colonial expansion. Developments in agriculture and trade led to divisions within the population of well-established states: landowners found themselves in conflict with the landless, those who lived within the city walls in tension with the communities living outside; old aristocracies defended their traditional privileges against new trade-created wealth. The enterprise of the Greek traders opened up the idea of new settlements and as colonies were established trade developed yet more, and standards of living rose. The economic changes induced political destabilization. As new states were founded around the shores of the Aegean, the Black Sea, and the Mediterranean, they needed their own constitutions. Some had imposed on them, or voluntarily adopted, the same constitution as their founder-state; others had new constitutions specially designed for them. In long-established states and new colonies alike older forms of government based on traditional hereditary kingships were frequently replaced by a new kind of leader whose position depended on the support of powerful interest groups within the state, not on kinship and descent.

The programme of colonial expansion coincided with the development of widespread literacy in the Greek world. The Greek alphabet provided a system of writing that made it possible for the first time in history for any reasonably intelligent person to acquire at least a basic knowledge of the skills of reading and writing. At first writing may have served as little more than a supplementary form of memory storage, but soon new forms of literature emerged exploiting the potentialities of written language. Early philosophical texts were to some extent of this kind, placing ideas, more or less systematically organized, before the reader who was now able not only to learn them, but also to read, reread, and study them.

Political and social conflict involves the struggle of ideas and values as much as armed combat and economic rivalry. Plato grew up in the midst of a major conflict between Athens and Sparta and a struggle within the city between oligarchic and democratic factions. There was, that is to say, a marked degree of plasticity in the political and social ideas current in Plato's Athens. Rival models were canvassed, opposing ideologies argued out in drinking circles and dinner parties as much as in the Assembly and the agora.

Plato was born at the end of an epoch. Four years before his birth Pericles had involved Athens in a disastrous war with Sparta which lasted almost thirty years and finally resulted in the utter humiliation of Athens. In the same year that the Peloponnesian war broke out, a terrible plague attacked Attica and during the next four years killed off up to a third of the entire population.

Pericles died in 429 depriving the city of its living symbol of political stability and military ascendancy and leaving it to meet the military and political challenge of Sparta under increasingly insecure leadership. Plato's childhood, youth, and early adult life were passed in a city at war. The social position and political interests of his close relatives meant that the politics and the military issues of the war were of intense interest in his home.

When Plato was about 5 years old, the Athenians retook Skione, a city in Chalkidike which had defected to the Spartan side. Athens put to death the entire male population of Skione, and sold all of its women and children into slavery. Six years later, the island of Melos refused to ally itself with Athens. Even though Melos was prepared to be neutral, the Athenians besieged the city, captured it, and subjected it to the same appalling fate as Skione.

To his undying credit, the tragedian Euripides had the courage to thrust before the eyes of his fellow citizens the agony they had brought upon the women of Melos, portraying them as the widowed and captive victims of the Trojan war in his grim play *The Trojan Women*. The theatre in classical Athens was not merely a place of entertainment. The great contests in which the dramatists competed had powerful religious overtones. The plays they produced explored in concrete images the ultimate problems of human existence; the subjection of humanity to the blind forces of fate, the conflict between personal duty and the power of the state, the hopeless misery of the victims of war and power politics, the self-perpetuating and futile dynamism of the feud, the whimsy and the unfeeling cruelty of the gods, the desperate human thirst for certainty, the fragile but creative beauty of compassion. In his later years Plato was to show himself resolutely hostile to the freedom of dramatists to sway their audiences' thoughts and feelings. The strength of his opposition is testimony to the power he recognized the drama to possess.

The year 415 marked the beginning of a vast military expedition to Sicily. The forces set out under the leadership of the great general Nicias, whose enthusiasm for the enterprise must have been somewhat limited. Their departure was clouded by a bizarre act of sacrilege; in one night all the sacred Herms in Athens were broken. The omen was accurate: the Athenians struggled for two years to take Syracuse; despite the commitment of tens of thousands of men, immense numbers of ships, and huge resources of armaments, the Athenian force underwent a crushing defeat that left Nicias himself dead, about seven thousand prisoners languishing in the quarries of Syracuse, and many more sold into slavery. This defeat happened when Plato was about 14 years old.

In 411 the democracy was overthrown by a right-wing revolution. A Council of Five Hundred took power, but managed to hold it for only two years. The democracy was restored and the war continued. Despite opportunities to negotiate a peace from which at least some vestiges of the Athenian empire could have been salvaged, the rhetoric of crass jingoism won the day and Athens committed itself to fighting out the war to the bitter end.

The end was bitter. In the spring of 404, when Plato was 23, the city was forced to capitulate. The capture of its fleet and of thousands of soldiers, and a harsh winter of disease and starvation under close siege had brought the city to its knees. The citizens waited in terror while the Spartans and their allies debated what should be done with them and with their city. Memories of the outrages of Skione and Melos had not faded; with good reason many Athenians must have feared they might be offered a sharp dose of their own inhuman medicine. There were indeed powerful voices amongst the Spartan allies to argue for such a final solution. In the end, however, Athens was granted Spartan mercy: the people were spared, but their Long Walls, the main defence works of Athens, were torn down and the democracy abolished to make way for a government of thirty rulers carefully selected for their anti-democratic and pro-Spartan attitudes.

No doubt there were many thoughtful men of Plato's class who shed few tears at the passing of the democracy. They may well have hoped for a return to stability and prosperity under a leadership drawn from their own educated, respectable, and wealthy circles. Plato certainly did. The Thirty included men of his own family, men who had frequented the company of Socrates honing their political ideas against the whetstone of his analytical mind. Tragic as the defeat was, it had opened up the city to radical political and social reforms. Plato was at 23 an intelligent man with a genuine enthusiasm for political reform. He had learned from Socrates a thoroughgoing contempt for a 'democratic' system whose highest offices were allocated by lottery, and which had shown itself in the later stages of the war disquietingly vulnerable to the persuasive voices of irresponsible demagogues. Plato may very possibly have experienced the realities of military service. It is certain he would have attended debates in the Assembly and learned at first hand the realities of decision making under the democracy. He would have visited the law courts too. Legal cases were a major focus of popular interest in Athens not least since politicians could be made or broken in a law suit.

With the appointment of the Thirty, Plato looked forward to a period of rational government by able, intelligent, and virtuous men who embodied the sound values and deeply embedded sense of duty of his own aristocratic class. Plato's disillusionment was swift and total. The rule of the Thirty was bloody and immoral. Under the leadership of his great-uncle Critias the Thirty Tyrants instituted a reign of terror: their opponents perished, potential opponents perished, and estates were sequestrated. To Plato's intense disgust, the Thirty even attempted to incriminate Socrates in their actions by involving him in the arrest of one of their victims.

Surviving supporters of the democracy fled and organized a revolutionary force under the generals Thrasybulus and Anytus. When the Spartans failed to come to the aid of the Thirty, in 403 they forced their way back into the city and restored the democracy. The restoration was carried out with quite extraordinary restraint. For a moment it must have seemed to a young man like Plato that at last the sober and upright rule of law and political good sense which the Thirty, despite all their talk of virtue, had so signally failed to bring about, might become a reality under the moderate government of the restored democracy. When in 399 the new democratic regime put Socrates to death, Plato was left embittered and deeply hurt. He laid aside any ambitions he had for an active involvement in Athenian politics and committed himself to the study of philosophy.

During his youth Plato had already followed his uncles Charmides and Critias and his brothers Adeimantus and Glaucon into the company of Socrates. He now retired with other members of Socrates' circle to stay at Megara with Euclides, an Eleatic philosopher who had been present at Socrates' death.

Socrates was something of a civic institution in Athens during Plato's youth. He was a familiar figure in the public places of the city; his fellow citizens were well used to seeing him in the agora, at the gymnasium, or walking about the city surrounded by a cluster of young men and a scattering of older friends and companions, immersed in conversation.

There is a famous story that his friend Chaerophon was told by the Delphic Oracle that there was no one 'more free, more just, or more wise' than Socrates, and that the oracle inspired Socrates, convinced as he was that he knew nothing, to search for someone who was indeed wiser and more knowledgeable than he was. Having found, despite the confident presumption of those of his fellow citizens whom he questioned, that no one in Athens knew more than the nothing he knew, Socrates is said to have concluded he was indeed the wisest man in the city, since he at least knew that he knew nothing.

Socrates seems, however, to have been impressed with the skill of the craftsmen he met. He is portrayed as returning time and time again to the example of the craftsman to point to the egregious absurdity of relying on experts to make our shoes, our pots, and our weapons while allowing an Assembly of amateurs to make our laws. He used the evident skill of the craftsman as a model for the practical knowledge which enables the person who possesses it to lead a virtuous life.

Several of Socrates' associates, Antisthenes and Aristippus for example, were themselves to become celebrated philosophers, and in some cases founders of schools of philosophy. It is a testimony to Socrates' success as a teacher that, although his associates were united in sharing his interest in questions of value, their theoretical standpoints differed considerably.

Socrates was never a professional teacher, but he was ready to make use of the techniques of verbal combat the Sophists had developed and to apply them to a serious philosophical purpose, turning the question-and-answer game the Sophists used as an exhibition piece to demonstrate their skills into a strategy for the conversational destruction-testing of definitions.

Socrates won the devotion and loyalty of many of his associates; he also won the suspicion and hostility of many of his fellow citizens. Some were no doubt influenced by the absurd caricature of Socrates in Aristophanes' play *The Clouds*, where he appears in his Thinkery, as a bizarre eccentric constructing abstruse speculations on natural philosophy, whilst suspended in mid air in a basket. To anyone who knew him the portrait was, as it was intended to be, preposterous; to someone who knew him by name and rumour and no more, the caricature might well be taken for the truth. To those who resented his contempt for the democracy, and to those who were deeply suspicious of his open association with such notorious persons as Critias and Alcibiades, he would have appeared a dangerous word-spinner who taught clever young men how to put one over on their elders and betters by making the weaker case seem the stronger. To those who saw him with such hostile eyes, it cannot have been surprising that soon after the restoration of the democracy he was put on trial.

At exactly what point Plato began to write and publish we do not know. It seems unlikely that he produced any of the works we know during Socrates' lifetime, though there is no reason to believe he had written nothing at all before Socrates' death. He may well have committed to writing thoughts, impressions, arguments, and philosophical ideas which are reflected in his published dialogues but which would originally have been noted down for his own use or for discussion with friends. What is clear is that the need to defend the memory of Socrates against his detractors would have been a factor that influenced his decision to publish.

Plato soon became known as a philosopher in his own right. The Socratic dialogues he published were more than mere memoirs, they were also serious pieces of philosophical discussion, albeit presented in a lively and entertaining literary form.

In 388 BCE, at about the age of 40, Plato visited Italy and Sicily. His visit was of great importance for two reasons: Plato made the acquaintance of Archytas of Tarentum, the major living representative of the Pythagorean school and he formed a lasting friendship with Dion, the brother-in-law of Dionysius I, tyrant of Syracuse. The first of these relationships opened Plato to a powerful intellectual influence which provided exactly the stimulus he needed to generate his own systematic response to the diet of questions he had inherited from Socrates. The second led to two later visits to Syracuse in 367 and 361. On these two occasions Plato attempted with a quite singular lack of success to turn the young tyrant Dionysius II into the kind of ruler he and Dion felt the state needed. He started by teaching Dionysius the elements of geometry and he got no further.

Soon after his return from his first visit to Syracuse, Plato founded the Academy. Legally the Academy was a religious association; in reality it was a college of scholars, teachers, and students working together, dedicated to philosophical and scientific study. The rest of Plato's life, apart from his brief and futile involvement in the politics of Syracuse, was spent studying and teaching in the Academy and in producing the body of published works we now possess.

The Academy became the intellectual home of distinguished scholars. Its mathematical and philosophical attainments were famous. Some work was also done in other scientific fields such as biology and medicine. In 367, the year of Plato's second visit to Syracuse, Aristotle came to join the Academy. He arrived as a young man of 19 and remained there until Plato's death.

Plato died at 80 years of age. He had never married. His works demonstrate the importance of friendship in Plato's life. He spent all the latter years of his life as an active member of an intellectual community respected as its founder, reverenced as the successor of Socrates, and loved as a man of unique wisdom, learning, and virtue.

2
Plato's writings

Plato's writings are the best and most reliable source we possess for our knowledge of his thought and his work as a philosopher; they are however a problematic source.

With the exception of the *Letters* and the *Apology* they are in the form of dialogues. Some are true dialogues, some virtually monologues sprinkled with interjections. The interpretation of them as evidence for Plato's own views is no easy matter. In most of the dialogues Socrates is the principal speaker, though in dialogues of Plato's latest period he fades in importance, and in the *Laws* is replaced by an Athenian stranger who lacks any dramatic reality. Knowing the reverence with which Plato regarded Socrates it is tempting to see the dialogues where Socrates does appear as a naturalistic portrayal of Socrates and to conclude that what Socrates argues in the dialogues represents the opinions and arguments of the historical Socrates. Unfortunately, this view is not tenable in face of the clear and explicit testimony of Aristotle that Socrates never held certain doctrines Plato has him expound at length in the dialogues.

Equally there is a problem in accepting Socrates as always simply playing the role of Plato's mouthpiece. In some of the dialogues Socrates deploys transparently fallacious arguments: it seems difficult to accept that Plato accepted such arguments as valid when writing the dialogues. In the *Protagoras* Socrates is made to engage in an elaborate and quite absurd piece of poetical exegesis. It is hard to believe that Plato approved of such forms of activity and that he is using Socrates to present a model example.

It is in general unsafe to assume that the arguments and ideas Plato puts into the mouth of Socrates are conclusive evidence for the arguments and ideas of the historical Socrates; it is almost as unsafe to assume without further supporting evidence that they represent the views of Plato either. That is not, of course, to say there is no significant link between the Socrates of the dialogues and the historical Socrates, nor is it to deny that on the whole the opinions and arguments Plato puts into the mouth of Socrates are more likely to represent Plato's views than are those he puts into the mouths of most other speakers in the dialogues. There are, however, specific passages in the dialogues where it is evident from the nature, form, and content of the discussion that a speaker other than Socrates is Plato's mouthpiece. The most obvious case of this is presented by the arguments of Parmenides in the dialogue named after him; it is clearly Parmenides rather than Socrates who represents Plato's position in at least a major part of the dialogue.

The more the dialogue in which Socrates is engaged is a genuine dialogue, and the more the structure of that dialogue is shaped by a genuine interplay of contrasting views and arguments, the more it is the dialogue itself, rather than Socrates as an individual character within it, that is the spokesman of Plato. The more the dialogue form collapses into a mere routine, where Socrates dominates the conversation totally, leaving his interlocutors to do little more than interject occasional and quite dispensable banalities, the more we can feel safe in taking Socrates to be the mask through which Plato speaks.

Plato was not the only author of Socratic dialogues. When the restored democracy put Socrates to death, it gave birth to a new literary form. A number of his former associates created a whole literature of dialogues in which Socrates was the principal character. Sadly, except for fragments, the entirety of this literature is lost except for those dialogues which have come down to us under the names of Plato and Xenophon. There are, of course, later examples of the form, and the Platonic corpus includes spurious dialogues, some of which are very early and which, while not directly useful to the interpretation of Plato, are of some interest in themselves.

The Socratic literature included works hostile to Socrates: the sophist Polycrates, for example, wrote a celebrated version of Anytus' speech for the prosecution, justifying the execution of Socrates.

Xenophon wrote a number of Socratic dialogues. Like Plato
he wrote an *Apology* presenting Socrates defending himself at his
trial. He wrote a *Symposium* which, while it lacks the dramatic
and philosophical brilliance of Plato's dialogue of the same
name, is none the less an enjoyable, lively, and readable piece. He
consciously and overtly wrote the *Memorabilia*, a lengthy collection of reminiscences, anecdotes, and conversations, to defend
Socrates against the calumnies directed against him. He wrote to
describe and defend Socrates' way of life, to extol and exemplify
his virtues.

Xenophon's Socrates is more down-to-earth, more overtly a
moralist, more harsh on occasion, than Plato's. There is, however, a significant degree of overlap between the two portraits:
both sets of dialogues show us a man deeply interested in questions of morality and of values; both show him using the technique of systematic questioning to test the truth of the answers his
interlocutors propose; both show him reasoning by analogy from
the skills of craftsmen; both show a man whose conversation
flickers with engaging touches of humour and wit. The Socrates
of Xenophon as much as the Socrates of Plato surrounds himself
with intelligent, questioning friends who share his enthusiasm
for philosophical discussion. Both portray him as the enemy of
irrational forms of government and of immoral and foolish
conduct in personal as in public life.

Although he sometimes uses Socrates as the mouthpiece for his
own interests (in military theory, for example, or domestic eco-
nomy), Xenophon's Socratic dialogues are fundamentally biographical in purpose: he aims to present the life, the conversation,
the ideas, the religious beliefs, the personal relationships of
Socrates in such a way as to refute accusations which have been
made against him. Some of Plato's dialogues share something
of this purpose, the *Apology* most explicitly. Most of Plato's
dialogues, however, are fundamentally concerned with philosophical questions; any biographical interest they have is secondary. They are intended for study. The dialogues of Xenophon
are a useful corrective to any temptation we might have to read
the Platonic dialogues as records of actual conversations between
Socrates and the other characters who appear in them; at the

same time they serve to confirm the reliability of certain elements in the portrait of Socrates we find in the Platonic dialogues. In general, where Xenophon's works directly confirm the evidence of Plato's, it is reasonably safe to follow them both; when the evidence of the two authors is in conflict, it is not safe to follow either without additional supportive evidence from another source.

Plato was a philosopher. That has frequently been understood to imply that he was a man with a philosophy, a fixed set of doctrines he held consistently throughout his working life. His works are then read from the standpoint of the assumption that they all present a single, immutable, cohesive body of teachings. Such a reading of Plato's works is a gross over-simplification. Once we put aside any such prejudice and read the dialogues in the light of the evidence modern scholarship has produced as to the historical order of Plato's writings, Plato is disclosed to us as a man of enquiring mind, open to new influences, ready to re-consider his position and to reconstruct the theoretical view he has tentatively established. He has a taste for fine arguments, and is as ready to subject his own views to destructive testing as an opponent's. His writings are an essential part of his activity as a philosopher: they reflect and embody the progress and develop-ment of his ideas.

It is not only his philosophical position that changes as he grows older: the dialogues show a clear shift in Plato's model of what philosophy is, and what it is to be a philosopher. They show new methods being applied, new techniques exploited. It is none the less the case that certain ideas are established and held with varying degrees of permanence during Plato's philosophical life. An early acquaintance with the ideas of Heraclitus left him per-manently distrustful of any attempt to ground claims to know-ledge on the evidence of sense-experience. He was influenced by Eleatic philosophy to seek an eternal, immutable, and intelligible ground to knowledge and to reality. He learned from Socrates the need to subject truth-claims to rigorous questioning and analysis. He followed the example of Socrates in seeking clear and coher-ent definitions of general terms, particularly of value terms. He inherited from Socrates a particular interest in the nature and the foundation of moral and political values. He inherited also a respect for dialectical methods, for the questioning and analysis of theoretical positions from within, in order to uncover the assumptions on which they are grounded.

The use of objective measures of style, of the chronological evidence provided by references to datable events which we find in the dialogues, and the possession of clear pieces of external testimony, such as that of Aristotle that the *Laws* is the last-written of Plato's works, have allowed scholars to construct convincing arguments for the relative dating of Plato's writings to the extent that in most cases the relative dating of the dialogues is no longer a matter of controversy (though specific problems of dating remain, especially the dating of the *Timaeus*).

A satisfactory system of relative dating does not of itself solve all our problems of interpretation. Knowing where a particular dialogue belongs in Plato's whole pattern of work does not immediately entail that Plato held any specific view expressed in it, or subscribed to any of the arguments used in it. Even if we conclude that Plato is indeed arguing for a particular view, it does not follow he held the same view ever after, any more than the lack of explicit reference to an idea or opinion in a particular dialogue implies Plato did not hold that particular view when writing that dialogue.

A particular problem is raised by the fact that there is still no complete scholarly agreement about the authenticity of certain works in the Platonic corpus. The *Letters* are particularly problematic; some scholars reject all of them and most scholars reject some of them. The Seventh Letter, however, has many defenders. It is a work of outstanding interest in that, if it is indeed genuine, it is in large part Plato's autobiography. The usual arguments from style are of little use to us in determining the claims of the letters to be genuine Platonic writings; they are so different from the dialogues in form, structure, and manner that stylistic comparisons are difficult to use as conclusive evidence. None the less, it seems reasonable to accept the basic, overall picture of the order of events in Plato's life described in the Seventh Letter as a basis for constructing his biography, since even if the letter is a forgery, it is clearly early in origin, and would have little point or plausibility if the general picture it painted were not true.

There is no complete agreement as to the genuineness of the two dialogues named after the sophist Hippias. Modern scholarship has veered rather to accepting them as genuine, but substantial doubts remain.

Apart from the dialogues themselves we have evidence for the nature of Plato's philosophical views from other writers, particularly from Aristotle. In some cases our sources explicitly declare Plato to have held positions for which there is no evidence in the dialogues. If the external evidence is to be believed, and when the source of it is Aristotle it seems reasonable to do so, then a question arises as to how we are to reconcile the evidence for the unwritten doctrines Plato is said to have taught with the evidence for his philosophical activities presented in his published works.

It is obvious that Plato's philosophical activity was not limited to the writing and publication of the dialogues. He was an eminent teacher and inevitably in his teaching practice must have dealt with ideas and arguments which find little or no reflection in the published works. It is also by no means impossible that Plato believed that some of his philosophical results should be treated with a degree of reserve. A modern philosopher is likely to find such a position inappropriate and even reprehensible, but it was quite certainly the view of the Pythagorean school which exercised a considerable influence on Plato's development.

Interpreting Plato involves us in time-travel: it would be foolish to assume that because Plato was a philosopher his principal intellectual concerns were necessarily those of a philosopher of our own day. Fourth-century Athens presented him with problems quite other than those which order the conversation of a twentieth-century Oxford common-room. He was a teacher and the head of an academic institution; but the Academy, whilst in some ways it has claims to be considered the first University in Europe, was an institution quite different in kind from anything in our contemporary society.

A contemporary philosopher is likely to come to Plato's works looking for subtle analytic arguments, for logical insights, for examples of the analysis of concepts, of the unpackaging of the implications of specific linguistic uses, for examinations of the truth-claims of theories and of their testing for consistency and for internal and mutual coherence, for discussion of the ultimate grounds of claims to knowledge, and for the application of the results of such discussion to particular cases. The reader who comes with such expectations will not be disappointed; Plato's writings are rich in examples of philosophical work of this kind, and some of it is of astonishing originality and sophistication. There is, however, much that a modern reader does not expect to find in a work of philosophy. For example, there are passages which present not arguments but myths, stories resting on the authority of priests, priestesses, or sages, which present ideas for which no further proof is offered, but which seem to be of great importance to the development of the argument in particular dialogues. There are elaborate passages of literary parody, complex and clearly fallacious arguments the fallacious quality of which passes without comment. There are occasions when Plato seems to be expending considerable effort tearing down an intellectual construction he has recently been at great pains to erect. There are works and sections of works marked with an almost mystical tone, passages that Neo-Platonists and early Christians alike used as the basis for systems of spiritual teaching. There are lengthy passages of speculative political, social, economic, and educational theorizing which a modern philosopher of the analytic tradition may feel have virtually nothing to do with philosophy, but which for Plato are evidently of such central importance to what he thought his work as a philosopher to be that they fill his last work, the *Laws*, and constitute his intellectual testament.

Plato philosophized in a period when the various intellectual activities which history was to resolve into separate academic disciplines distinct in object-matter and method were generally not yet separated and articulated. The fundamental concepts with which he deals, and the distinctions that lie at hand in his own culture for his use, represent a stage in the history of ideas marked by a much higher level of conceptual plasticity than that to which the modern reader is accustomed. Frequently in translating Plato, one is faced with a baffling choice of English terms each of which captures some, and none of which captures all, of the meaning of a particular Greek word he uses.

It is possible to approach Plato from the point of view of our contemporary philosophical interests and concerns, and doing so can lead to interesting and useful interpretative discussions of his works. Unfortunately one pays the price for such an approach of losing Plato as he was: one substitutes for the historical Plato with his sometimes odd and uncomfortable concerns a sterilized and unhistorical figure who would be much more at home in a contemporary University department than would the author of the *Laws*.

3

Early dialogues: the *Laches*

In this chapter the form, content, and philosophical concerns of Plato's early dialogues are illustrated by means of an examination of the *Laches*. The *Laches* is one of the most accessible of the early dialogues. Typically, it is a lively and lifelike conversational piece. Socrates is drawn into a discussion between the two famous generals Nicias and Laches and their friends Lysimachus and Melesias, who have approached the two generals to ask their advice on the education of their young sons. Laches suggests they should ask the advice of Socrates, since he is a man of their own deme, has a considerable interest in all those things that are suitable pursuits and studies for young men, and is a man to whose courage Laches can testify from personal experience. Nicias seconds his suggestion, saying Socrates found him a good music teacher for his son. The suggestion is accepted, and the serious business of the dialogue begins.

Lysimachus asks Socrates whether he thinks boys should learn armoured combat. At Socrates' suggestion, Nicias gives his view first: it is a good and healthy activity, particularly appropriate for free citizens and useful preparation for battle; it will give them an interest in learning to lead troops, and thus in generalship; a knowledge of armoured combat will make one braver in battle.

Laches disagrees. If it were truly an accomplishment and not something trivial and worthless, it would indeed be worth studying. He doubts, however, the value of training in armoured combat since the professors of martial arts who specialize in this form of training are notable for their avoidance of Sparta, the city where the arts of war are most avidly pursued. The only expert Laches has actually seen in a genuine fight, a man called Stesilaus, took part in a fight on board a ship wielding a spear-scythe, a new-fangled weapon of his own invention, and ended up with his peculiar weapon ignominiously entangled in the rigging. Above all he dissents from Nicias' view on the ground that if the person who learned armoured combat was a coward to start with, it would merely make him foolhardy, while if he was a brave man, he would become an object of jealousy and others would be continually on the watch for his slightest mistake.

Lysimachus now asks Socrates (184 d) to decide between the two opposing pieces of advice: 'We ought to hear you too, Socrates,' he says, 'to find who you vote with!'

'What's this, Lysimachus,' Socrates answers, 'are you going to follow the majority vote?'

'What else would one do?'

'And you, Melesias, is this what you would do? Suppose you were taking advice about the sort of exercises your son should be performing to prepare himself for a competition; would you take guidance from the majority of us or from that one person who should happen to have been trained by and have exercised under a good trainer?'

Not surprisingly Melesias opts for the latter.

The question Socrates puts to Lysimachus and Melesias recurs in various forms in many dialogues. Socrates continually opposes the reasonableness of relying on expert knowledge to the irrational habit of following the crowd. 'Sound judgement', he says, 'is based on knowledge, not on numbers.' The question is not, for Socrates, who can command the majority vote, but which of us is relevantly expert in the matter under discussion.

The problem now is to determine exactly what kind of expert we should be looking for in order to provide Lysimachus and Melesias with the advice they are seeking:

'Well, surely, Socrates,' says Nicias, 'we are thinking about armoured combat and whether young men ought to learn it.'

'Indeed, Nicias, but suppose someone was considering whether a particular drug is a suitable eye ointment or not: would the object of these deliberations be the drug or the eyes?'

'The eyes.'

'And if one were considering whether or not, a horse ought to be bridled, and, if so, when, it is the horse one would be thinking about, not the bridle?'

'Yes.'

'In a word, then, whenever anyone thinks about one thing for the sake of another, what he is really concerned with is the end he has in mind, rather than the means to it.'

In the present case, what is really under discussion is what Plato calls the soul and what in this case we would probably call the character or the personality of the young men. The boys' fathers need to find an expert in soul-therapy, in character-formation, if they are to get good advice.

The move Socrates has made has shifted the discussion from its original focus on whether or not armoured combat is worth studying to a very different question: where are we to find expertise in character-formation? He accomplishes the shift by insisting the discussion is really about ends, not merely the means to them. Before we can give any worthwhile answer to questions about the educational value of the study of armoured combat, we need to know what our aim is in educating the young. He insists, that is, in grounding the original question under discussion in a more fundamental question, the answer to which will furnish the necessary rationale for the original question's being worthy of consideration at all. We start with a question about armoured combat, and to answer it we might be tempted to turn to an expert in the martial arts; we now are faced with a much deeper question about the aims of education, the objectives of character-formation, and need a quite different kind of expert to help us, not merely an expert in educational methods, but rather someone who combines that expertise with a knowledge of the ultimate aims education ought to serve. We need an expert in educational methods who is also an expert in human values.

In Plato's Athens there certainly existed a class of men who proclaimed themselves to be educational experts of such a kind. The Sophists claimed to be teachers of virtue, inculcators of excellence. They claimed to improve their students, to make them better persons than they formerly were. As will be evident when we come to look at the *Gorgias* and the *Protagoras*, Plato treated the educational pretensions of the Sophists with contempt, and as the years passed his contempt increased. But he was fascinated by the philosophical problem their claims raised: can virtue be taught? What kind of teaching makes someone a better person?

Who is the expert in virtue? Who has the knowledge required to teach others how to excel as human beings? How can such knowledge be acquired?

'Well now, Laches,' says Socrates (190 b), 'these two are surely inviting us to consider in what way virtue might be imparted to their sons and their characters thereby improved.' For this to be possible, as Socrates points out, it is necessary to know what virtue is. He suggests the enquiry into the nature of virtue should begin with one part of it, courage, since this will be easier than attempting to investigate the whole of virtue at once. Besides, courage is the part of virtue that the practice of armoured combat is supposed to develop.·

What Socrates is saying implies, of course, that virtue is a whole of which courage is a part. It is not safe to assume that Plato is using this formulation as more than a working proposition in the context of a particular argument. The nature of the discussion in the *Laches* is itself sufficient evidence that Plato had a sophisticated awareness of the problem of relating individual virtue-concepts such as courage and prudence to the concept of virtue as such. The distinctions a modern philosopher has at hand between being a member of a class, being a subset of a set, being a part of a whole, and being an individual of which a predicate is predicated, had not been formulated in Plato's day. His use of the language of part–whole relations must not, then, be taken as a sign of such a distinction unless there is some clear indication that this is what Plato intends. The debate on the nature of virtue, and on the nature of one particular virtue, courage, that forms the substance of the *Laches*, raises the question of the nature of the relation of one virtue to another, and of the relation between individual virtues and virtue itself.

Socrates now asks for a definition of courage. 'Heavens, that's not difficult, Socrates,' says Laches, 'a man who is ready to stand his post, faces the enemy, and doesn't run away, he would certainly be courageous.' This, as Socrates points out, will not do; it is an instance, not a definition. What he is asking for is not an example of courage, but a statement of what courage is in every possible instance. He gives an example of the kind of definition he is looking for. He takes the example of quickness, and points to a range of instances of it. Then he says: 'Suppose someone asked me, "Socrates, what is this that you call quickness in every instance?" I should answer that what I call quickness, whether in running, speaking, or any other case, is the capacity to do much in a little time.' This model definition indicates what kind of formula Socrates is looking for as a definition of courage: he is looking for a formula which specifies the nature of courage, which tells us what courage essentially is in itself and in every instance that we apply the term 'courage' to something.

Elsewhere in the early dialogues Socrates is made to formulate similar questions by asking what is the *eidos*, the form, shape, or pattern of something. In the *Euthyphro*, for instance, when Socrates on his way to be tried ends up in conversation with Euthyphro, a professional religious expert, and questions him as to the nature of piety, he puts the question like this (6 d): 'Then recall that this isn't what I asked for, for you to inform me about one or two of the many cases of piety, but rather this, the very form [*eidos*] according to which every pious thing is pious . . .'

Laches offers a definition of courage: 'Then I take courage to be a kind of steadfastness of spirit if I am to talk about what is common to all cases.'

Socrates now examines Laches' definition by means of questioning him. The technique he uses is a conversational adaptation of a debating technique used by the Sophists. They had developed a form of verbal combat by questioning in which one speaker propounded a thesis and his opponent sought to reduce him to self-contradiction or to silence by systematically questioning him. The technique may well have been developed from a particular feature of Athenian legal procedure, which permitted a litigant to subject his opponent to a stream of questions expecting simple yes/no answers. The Sophists worked up a highly stylized version of the question–answer session, presenting formal word-battles with a time limit and a referee. Such word-battles, while they could degenerate into the most vapid and futile exercises in verbal gymnastics based on systematic equivocation, when skilfully fought by combatants ready to argue out the merits of a thesis of some intrinsic interest provided an impressive exhibition of the speakers' debating skills. Socrates realized that the

systematic questioning of a proposition could be used to test its
consistency; if the series of questions can bring the defender of
the proposition under discussion to infer from it contradictory
conclusions, then, if the inferences are valid, the proposition is
refuted. In Socrates' hands the method of question and answer
gains a particular power since he is careful to conduct the whole
argument on the basis of positions genuinely accepted by his interlocutor. The effect of this is that when the interlocutor's position is
eventually refuted, he feels a real sense of bafflement, not merely
resentment at the cleverness of his questioner.

Laches has defined courage as steadfastness. Socrates raises a
query as to whether every instance of steadfastness is an instance
of courage.

'I am sure, Laches, you would hold that courage is a fine
thing?'

'Amongst the finest of things, for sure.'

'And steadfastness combined with wisdom is something fine
and good?'

'Indeed.'

'But what if it is combined with foolishness? Would not that be
something bad and harmful?'

'Yes.'

'And are you prepared to call something bad and harmful a
fine thing?'

'No, Socrates, that would not be right.'

'Then you would not admit that such a kind of steadfastness is
courage, since courage is a fine thing, and this is not?'

'You are right.'

Courage and steadfastness cannot, that is to say, be identical,
since courage is always something fine, whereas steadfastness is
not. Steadfastness or persistence is an ethically neutral capacity,
and courage a virtue, although the two may be easy to confuse.

The refutation turns upon a logical law, unformulated in
Plato's day, but presupposed by many of the arguments in the
dialogue, that if A is logically identical with B, then whatever is
true of A is true of B and whatever is true of B is true of A. The
demonstration that something is true of A but not of B is proof
that A is not identical to B.

Having refuted Laches' suggestion that courage is steadfastness, Socrates infers from the argument he has just constructed that Laches might now prefer to say courage is wise steadfastness. Laches assents. Socrates immediately demolishes this definition in turn by pointing out the very different activities in respect of which one can be wisely steadfast, and asking Laches whether he accepts every case as one of courage. Since the cases include such things as being wisely steadfast in one's financial affairs, or, in the case of a doctor, in refusing a patient's request for food and drink which would harm him, Laches is forced to admit that not every case of wise steadfastness is a case of courage.

Socrates now asks Laches which of two men he would regard as the more courageous, one who in a battle fights steadfastly on, wisely calculating that others are about to come to his aid and that the forces which oppose him will be fewer and weaker than his own, and who has in addition the advantage of position, or a man in the enemy force who stands steadfastly against him.

'The opponent, I should say, Socrates.'

'But is not the steadfastness of this man more unwise than that of the other?'

'You are right.'

'And in a cavalry engagement, you would say an expert horseman who behaves steadfastly shows less courage than one who has no knowledge of horsemanship?'

'I think I would.'

'And a man who has knowledge of the sling-shot or the bow or any other such skill, and who behaves steadfastly?'

'Indeed.'

'And someone who descends a well, or dives and who does so steadfastly, or anything else of the kind, and who has no expertise in such things, would you not say he showed more courage than an expert who did the same?'

'What else is one to say, Socrates?'

'Nothing, if that's what he thinks!'

'Well that is what I think.'

'But people who hazard themselves in this way and are steadfast in doing so are foolish by comparison with those who have the proper skills for the task.'

'Obviously.'

'But earlier on foolish boldness and steadfastness seemed to us to be base and harmful?'

'Indeed.'

'Whereas we acknowledged courage to be something fine?'

'Quite so.'

'And now on the contrary we are saying that a base thing, foolish steadfastness, is courage!'

'So it seems.'

'And do you think we are right in saying this?'

'God forbid, Socrates. We are certainly not right.'

Laches is baffled. His attempt at a definition of courage has collapsed in absurdity. As Socrates says, their words and deeds are in discord; their actions show they both have their share of courage, but their discussion has failed to grasp what it is. We face a paradox; Laches and Socrates are both men of proven bravery, whatever courage might be they both possess it, but so far they seem unable to decide what it is.

Socrates suggests they press on steadfastly with their enquiry. Laches is keen to do so; he is irritated at his failure to express his thoughts: 'I seem to intuit in some way what courage is, but when I try to put it into words, it gives me the slip!' Laches is experiencing *aporia*, bewilderment. The self-contradiction into which Socrates' questions have led him has both roused his interest and left him utterly confused. This is for Plato a healthful state. Before the conversation that has just taken place, Laches no doubt existed in that confident state of undiagnosed ignorance that passes for common sense; now he has at least had his ignorance disclosed to him. The mental space has been cleared that is the prerequisite of all learning: Laches' hitherto untested assumptions about courage have been put to the test, found inconsistent, and, given the basic reasonableness Laches shows, put aside. He now has discovered he does not know something he presumed he knew; he is both irritated and fascinated by the discovery, and motivated by an ambition to solve the problem of finding a correct definition of courage.

Socrates now invites Nicias to join the discussion. From the conversation it is evident that Nicias is already familiar not only with Socrates' methods but also with his philosophical ideas: 'I've been thinking for a while, Socrates, that you are not defining courage in the right way. I heard a fine saying of yours that you're neglecting.'

'And what was that, Nicias?'

'I have often heard you say a man is good in those things about which he is wise, and bad in things of which he is ignorant.'

The remark Nicias has quoted represents one aspect of Socrates' well-known, if paradoxical, belief that virtue is knowledge. The basic idea underlying this may be that virtue is excellence and that to excel we need to be able to do things exceptionally well, and that to do something well we need knowledge and expertise. The suggestion that there is a strong cognitive element to virtue, and especially to moral or civic virtue, comes as a surprise to many modern readers of Plato, who frequently assume virtue is a matter of intention or attitude or sentiment. Such readers of Plato find Socrates' persistent belief that virtue is knowledge of some kind utterly bizarre, and the paradoxical belief he also defends, that no one knowingly or willingly does wrong, perverse and absurd. For Socrates, all vice is essentially error, all wrong doing a mistake. That does not mean he regards evil actions lightly; on the contrary, it is why he shares with Plato a passionate interest in education.

'What I should say, Laches, is that courage is the knowledge of what is to be dreaded and what is confidence-inspiring both in war and in everything else.' Laches is unwilling to accept Nicias' definition, since it seems to him to confuse courage with wisdom and he sees these as clearly distinct. 'But that is what Nicias is explicitly denying,' says Socrates.

'Indeed he is,' says Laches, 'and he's talking piffle!'

'Well then, let's teach him, not abuse him!'

'It seems to me, Socrates, that Laches wants what I say to be proved to be nonsense, since that's exactly what's just happened to him.'

'Right you are, Nicias, and I'm going to have a go at proving it. You are talking nonsense. For instance, in the case of illnesses, isn't it doctors who know what is to be feared? Or is it your opinion that it's the courageous man who knows that? Or do you call doctors courageous?'

Laches' point seems apt. If courage is identical with knowledge of what is to be feared and what ought to inspire confidence, then the doctor's knowledge of what is to be feared in the case of illness must be an example of courage. Nicias' response is to make a distinction between the technical medical knowledge the doctor certainly has, and knowledge of another kind.

'Do you think, Laches, he knows which a man ought to fear more, recovery or remaining ill? Do you imagine this is something doctors know, Laches? Isn't it the case that many a man is better off if he never rises from his sickbed again than if he does? Tell me this: is it always better to live than to die? And isn't it often better to die?'

'Certainly, in my view.'

'And do you think the same things are to be feared by those for whom death would be better as by those who would be better off alive?'

'No, I don't.'

'And do you imagine a doctor possesses this knowledge, or any other expert, other than the person who knows what ought to be feared and what ought not? And that's the man I call courageous.'

Laches rejects this argument. It seems to him to make fortune-tellers and diviners courageous, since they are the people who claim the knowledge of the future which allows one to determine what should or should not be feared in a given case. Nicias replies that a fortune-teller might well know what was going to happen, but that that is not enough; he would need to know also whether the things he foresees ought to be accepted or avoided. Laches derides the whole argument Nicias is making as Nicias simply masking his own bewilderment behind empty words: 'In a court of law there might be some point to it, but in a gathering like this why this futile decking out of oneself with vacuous verbiage?'

The reader may well be left with the suspicion that there is more to Nicias' position than either Laches or Socrates has been willing to allow. Socrates himself now takes up the discussion again, pointing out one of the odder consequences of Nicias' argument.

If courage is a form of knowledge or wisdom, then it is never appropriate to call an animal courageous. Nicias accepts this; he is prepared to call an animal, or for that matter a child, fearless, rash, or bold, but since they act without forethought, he will not call them courageous.

Nicias' readiness to accept this particular move on Socrates' part betrays a certain *naïveté*. To defend his definition at the expense of common usage is a very expensive measure. If the definition can only be sustained at the expense of changing the use of the word defined, then it follows that the word which has been defined is not identical with the word originally under discussion. The new definition is revisionary and stipulative: it does not uncover the rationale for the existing use of the word, but proposes a new pattern of use. It is a problem Socrates himself would have to face, since if he persists in asserting that virtue is knowledge, then he too cannot attribute to an animal anything we would account a virtue unless he will allow that the animal has the knowledge which is what the virtue ultimately is.

Socrates now develops Nicias' argument in a new direction. He reminds the generals that they started out by separating out courage as one part of virtue; other parts exist—justice, *sophrosyne*, and so forth. (*Sophrosyne* is a difficult term to translate, it means self-restraint, balance, temperance, and moderation in one's conduct; soundness, thoughtfulness, and discretion in one's mental outlook.) All these taken together constitute virtue. Courage, in the light of Nicias' argument, would be the knowledge of the dreadful and of the confidence-inspiring. This cannot be knowledge merely of the future, it must be knowledge of the past and of the present also. In the end it must be a knowledge of good and evil. But the person who possessed the knowledge of good and evil would not merely have the kind of knowledge that Nicias has identified with courage; such a person would on the lines of his argument possess the whole of virtue, not merely a part.

This argument seems reasonable, since there seems no way of judging whether or not any particular outcome of a given situation is desirable or not unless one possesses a knowledge of the nature of the values which must be measured against each other to make that decision. One requires knowledge of what values are in order to make rationally grounded value judgements.

At this point it is clear the attempt to define courage has failed. The conversation draws to a close. Laches and Nicias are ready to leave the education of the boys to Socrates. He, however, is quick to point out (201 b) that throughout the conversation he has never shown any knowledge that the two generals did not possess: 'Let us not bother what people may say, but let us join together in furthering the boys' education, and our own!' The discussion of courage in the *Laches* is set in the context of an enquiry about how young men should best be educated. In the Athens of Plato's day there was an established pattern of education for the sons of the gentry. Skills of reading and writing were inculcated, as well as a thorough knowledge of poetic classics, of music, of athletics and gymnastics. An educated young man was expected to be a competent conversationalist, to carry himself well in society, to exhibit the virtues appropriate to his station, to know his duties as a member of his family, as a person moving in society, and as a citizen, to have a good knowledge of Homer and the poets, to appreciate music and to perform it competently, and to keep his body in sound physical condition by means of a well-designed programme of physical exercise. As he grew older, he might frequent specialist teachers to study mathematics, philosophy, rhetoric, or a range of other specialized disciplines; some aspect of the martial arts, for example, as in the *Laches*.

Plato directed a volley of dialogues against the pretension of those who have set themselves up as educators, especially against those who claim to teach virtue. He shared enough of Socrates' philosophical view to see an inadequate educational system, or still worse one which actually inculcated error, as morally debilitating or even depraving.

In the dialogue *Ion* Socrates questions a rhapsode, a professional reciter and exponent of Homer, who claims the works of Homer provide him with a wide knowledge of a variety of different kinds, from farming to military strategy. Socrates demonstrates clearly, though in such a way as to give little offence, that the intellectual pretensions of the rhapsode are empty. Homer's poetry is no source-book of encyclopaedic wisdom. The poet is not so much an artist, a man of knowledge and skill, as a man inspired, possessed. The critic is no expert on the topics the poet addresses unless he has made an actual study of them himself. Homer is inspired to write accounts of battles: the fact that a rhapsode can recite and expound his battle-passages does not turn him into an expert strategist or tactician, still less does it make him brave. The pretensions of poets, rhapsodes, and expositors of poetry to have knowledge or be seen as potential educators are left deflated.

The *Gorgias* explodes the claims of the *rhetor*, the professional orator and teacher of oratory, to teach virtue. Rhetoric, Socrates argues, is not an art, science, or skill but a mere knack. As dietetics is the science or art of nutrition, cookery is a knack of preparing food to titillate the palate. Rhetoric is the mere knack of serving up words to titillate the intellectual palate of an audience. This dialogue is almost certainly aimed quite directly at the rhetor Isocrates who opened a school of 'philosophy' about 388 BCE teaching the arts of rhetoric together with a thorough grounding in traditional values, based on the example of great men of the past. Such an education he thought adequate to the demands of public life. To Plato it would have seemed no more than a thorough soaking in untested opinions and prejudices, combined with a training in speech-making which in the absence of a sound educational grounding amounted to putting a powerful weapon in the hands of the irresponsible.

The *Protagoras*, the *Lesser Hippias*, and most significantly the *Euthydemus* challenge the pretensions of the sophists to teach virtue. The challenge is at a serious intellectual level in the *Protagoras*, and the great sophist himself is portrayed as a man of considerable character and intellectual accomplishments, however questionable his claims to teach virtue. The *Euthydemus* shows the horrendous results to which a sophistical education can lead. Euthydemus and Dionysodorus have undergone a thorough training in Word-Battle technique: in the dialogue they carry out a series of set-piece exchanges designed to reduce an interlocutor to baffled silence: he is offered alternative positions; whichever he holds he is refuted. There is no thirst for truth, no philosophical insight, no moral seriousness, nothing but well-rehearsed verbal tricks.

A brief example from the *Euthydemus* (283 c) will illustrate the nature and quality of the arguments the professional debaters use. Socrates recounts how Dionysodorus questioned him about what he wanted for the young man Cleinias:

' "Well then," he said, "you are saying you wish him to become wise?"

"Most certainly."

"And at the present moment," he went on, "is Cleinias wise or is he not?"

"He says he is not, as yet; he's no braggart!"

"And you wish him to become wise, not to be ignorant?"

We agreed.

"Well then, you wish him to become what he now is not, and to be no longer what he now is."

On hearing this I was confused. He took advantage of my confusion.

"Isn't it the case, then, that since you wish him no longer to be what he now is, that you evidently wish him to be annihilated!" '

Socrates offers a stinging critique of the word games Euthydemus and Dionysodorus play; he shows how they depend for their superficial success on the disputants' failing to distinguish different meanings of words, and how at the end of the day, while they may well manage to knock down the Aunt Sallies they have set up, they can never produce any positive result from their debates. He gives what is clearly Plato's own evaluation (278 b) of such exercises in equivocation and quibbling: 'Things like this are just playing at learning. That's why I say these men are merely playing with you. I say it's just playing because if you became very good at it, indeed if you became perfectly accomplished at all this, you would be no whit the wiser as to how things really are—all you'd have learned is how to make game of people, tripping them head over heels with verbal distinctions—just like someone pulling a stool away when a person's about to sit down and then howling with laughter when he sees him sprawling on his back.'

The *Laches* itself has already undermined any argument one might wish to raise on behalf of good men and true as educators: Laches and Nicias are the living embodiment of the virtue of courage, but neither can define what that virtue is. Laches feels he somehow intuits it, but cannot put it into words. Their failure is not due to stupidity, reluctance to try, nor to any lack of education or skill: both men show themselves in the dialogue to have genuine skill in debate, flexibility of mind, and a general sympathy for Socrates' intellectual quest as well as a personal respect for him. Nonetheless, they are not even in their own eyes suitable educators.

The outcome of Plato's philosophical investigations has so far proved somewhat alarming. All the plausible candidates to be considered as providers of an education suitable for the development of personal virtue and as preparation for undertaking the duties of citizenship have been decisively rejected. The portraits of Laches, Nicias, and Protagoras, even Gorgias despite his pompous manner, are all sympathetic: each comes across as a man with many fine personal and intellectual qualities. They represent the best the world has to offer as potential educators: it is not enough. Each attempt to grasp hold of a value term and define it has ended in failure: every time Socrates applies his question-test, the definitions proposed by his interlocutors collapse into inconsistency. Can it be true we do not know what courage is, what beauty is, what piety is?

If a contemporary reader submitted himself to the discipline of these dialogues, his intellectual self-confidence would surely have been radically undermined. The dialogues not only exhibit Socrates' interlocutors in a state of perplexed bewilderment, they are devices for inducing that state in the reader.

There are some hopeful traces. Socrates has provided us with a model of what an acceptable definition would look like, in his definition of quickness in the *Laches*. The sense Laches himself has that despite his failures to define courage he still has an intuition of what it is, is one the reader may well share. Something is still there, even if it has yet been brought to adequate verbal expression. Nicias' reminder to Socrates of his own maxim 'that each of us is good in matters wherein he is wise, bad in matters wherein he is unlearned' is also a pointer: our ignorance in matters of value is not total. We know there is an intimate relation between virtue and value and knowledge. What that relation is has so far not been uncovered, but the existence of such a relation is clear.

The discussions in the dialogues demonstrate Plato's confidence in the capacity of rational argument to operate effectively in the area of philosophical discussion. The early dialogues are in no way sceptical writings, they show the power of rational argument and systematic questioning to test opinions effectively. That the result is a massacre is testimony to the effectiveness of the test. It is also a testimony to the poor grounding even the most educated men have for their opinions.

4

Can virtue be taught: the *Protagoras*

The kinds of argument found in the *Laches* are typical of the arguments in the early dialogues. The question-testing of sequences of definitions is a common feature of a number of these dialogues: in the *Charmides* a definition of *sophrosyne* is sought, in the *Lysis* of friendship, in the *Greater Hippias* of beauty, in the *Euthyphro* of piety. Other dialogues raise and discuss a range of problems in the general field of morality and values. The *Crito*, for example, centres on a discussion of civic duty, the *Lesser Hippias* on the question whether it is better to do wrong intentionally or unintentionally. The early dialogues form a body of dialectical and analytical investigations of the nature of human values, the meaning of value expressions, and the logic of value language: they raise serious questions as to the nature and teachability of virtue. In the *Protagoras* and *Gorgias* the teachability of virtue is explored at length. The *Protagoras* focuses on the problem of the cognitive status of virtue, whether or not virtue is knowledge.

In an earlier age *arete* (virtue, excellence) was thought of by the aristocracy as their birthright. Good birth produced good men, naturally superior to the lower orders, innately suited for battle and debate. In the Athenian democracy, every citizen had military and political responsibilities: *arete* became a matter of fact and reputation—proven excellence on the battle field, a proven excellence in speechmaking and debate, a reputation for political influence, for wisdom and *sophrosyne*, for an ordered and honourable style of life. Not surprisingly enterprising men appeared, offering to teach excellence, to provide instruction in virtue. The outstanding representatives of this group were men of considerable intellectual ability and high reputation. The sophist Protagoras was eminent amongst them.

Protagoras was an able philosophical thinker and a noted

teacher. He seems to have taught a vigorous relativism, arguing that things are for each person as that person perceives and judges them to be. He seems to have sustained his claim to teach virtue, a paradoxical claim for so strict a relativist, by arguing that, although all opinions are equally true, none the less some are better than others. In a much later dialogue (the *Theaetetus*) Plato attempts to demonstrate that Protagoras' position is internally inconsistent. In the *Protagoras* it is not Protagoras' distinctive philosophical position that is at issue but rather his claim as a sophist to teach virtue and to improve those he teaches.

On a first reading the *Protagoras* seems to present a freely flowing discussion, meandering in a loosely structured way around questions concerning the nature and teachability of virtue. A closer reading discloses its complex structure. It also presents the reader with a number of puzzles: Socrates behaves in this dialogue in a quite irritating manner; he seems unnecessarily rude to Protagoras, he engages in nit-picking exegesis of poetry by Simonides, he bases a lengthy argument on hedonistic premises the historical Socrates certainly never held. Socrates and Protagoras seem to exchange positions in the dialogue, and the dialogue seems to leave the discussion at a completely unsatisfactory stage. In order to appreciate what Plato is doing in this dialogue, it is important to avoid the trap of seeing Socrates as simply Plato's mouthpiece: the Socrates of the *Protagoras* is a subtle literary creation, ironic, witty, and devious in argument, albeit always to a serious purpose. He puts on the mantle of the sophist to demonstrate how threadbare it is. Neither Socrates nor Protagoras should too easily be assumed to be the mouthpiece of Plato: it is the dialogue itself which represents Plato's thought, not merely one of the protagonists.

It would be possible to analyse the *Protagoras* in many different ways. Here is one possible analysis of the dialogue; it is presented at length because, despite being eminently readable, the dialogue has a complex and sometimes elusive structure. Constructing an analysis of the dialogue involves difficult decisions as to the function of specific parts of the conversation, and as to the relative importance of various elements. A reader of the dialogue who made the assumption that Socrates is Plato speaking through a mask would almost certainly analyse the dialogue in a quite different way, just as would a reader who thought an important function of the dialogue was to propose a hedonist view of values.

The Protagoras

A. Introduction

1. A conversation between Socrates and a friend: Socrates informs him he has just been talking to Protagoras. The friend asks for an account of the conversation.
2. Socrates recounts how Hippocrates had taken him to see Protagoras at the house of Callias: Hippocrates wishes to study with Protagoras. Socrates questions him: Why study with a sophist? A painter can teach painting, a sculptor sculpture; what has a sophist to teach? Surely Hippocrates does not wish to become a sophist himself? Perhaps the sophist offers no special form of learning, rather an advanced liberal education? Hippocrates assents. But what in the concrete does a sophist teach? Fine speaking? But on what subject? Socrates points out that Hippocrates is in danger of turning his soul (mind, character) over to a sophist without knowing what a sophist can actually do.
3. Socrates and Hippocrates arrive at the house of Callias and encounter Protagoras.

B. The First Debate: is virtue teachable?

Virtue and civic life

1. Protagoras' claim

Protagoras claims that if Hippocrates studies with him, he will go home a better man every day. Unlike other sophists who will teach him a variety of specialist subjects, Protagoras will teach him 'sound judgement in personal affairs so he can optimize the organization of his own household, and so far as civic affairs are concerned, maximize his effectiveness in speech and action' (319 a). Protagoras claims to teach the art of politics and to make men good citizens.

2. Socrates' refutation of 1

This, says Socrates, would be splendid if possible, but he argues that such things as civic virtue cannot be taught.

2.1. There are no specialists in civic virtue and politics: in the Assembly architects are consulted about building projects, naval architects about shipbuilding, but in matters of government every citizen has a voice. It follows that no one regards civic virtue as something which can be taught.

2.2. Virtuous men sometimes have vicious sons: if the best citizens cannot hand on their virtues to their own sons, then virtue must be unteachable.

3. Protagoras' defence of 1

3.1. His arguments are directed to showing all citizens of the *polis*, (the organised community, city, or State) have some measure of civic virtue.

3.1.1. Civic virtue is a necessary precondition of civic life. Protagoras uses the *myth of Prometheus and Epimetheus* to illustrate his argument that the kind of social life men have in the *polis* would be impossible without mutual respect and the sense of justice. All citizens must have a share of these, otherwise the structure of the *polis* would be unstable.

3.1.2. So (versus 2.1) it is no surprise that all citizens are listened to in matters of political decision: all have a share in the relevant virtue.

3.1.3. Anyone who confesses to wickedness is accounted mad: it would be folly to claim a technical skill—e.g. flute playing—if one does not possess it, but everyone is expected to claim a share of virtue.

3.2. Virtue is universal amongst citizens, but it is not innate.

3.2.1. No one is made angry by inborn faults or defects, but vicious conduct angers.

3.2.2. The institution of punishment shows virtue can be taught and vice corrected: punishment is educative either for the one punished or for others, otherwise it is brute vengefulness.

3.2.3. All education tends to the inculcation of virtue: domestic education and the study of the poets at school provide examples of virtue; musical study inculcates *sophrosyne* and opens up the teachings of the lyric poets. It has a generally balancing and civilizing influence, whilst physical education strengthens and helps avoid cowardice.

3.2.4. (versus 2.2) It is in everyone's interest to teach virtue to others. That some succeed better than others is because of the aptitudes of the learners. Even the poorest examples of virtue in the city are, however, paragons of virtue when compared to the brutish viciousness of savages.

3.3. There is an appropriate person to teach virtue: someone who is more advanced on the path of virtue than his pupil, and that is all Protagoras claims to be.

C. *The Second Debate: is virtue teachable?*

Are all virtues one? Is knowledge part of all virtues, even of courage?

4. Socrates' question

Are all the names of the virtues merely different names for one and the same thing, or are they names of different parts of virtue?

4.1. *Protagoras' reply*

The virtues are distinct, they differ as the parts of the face, each having its own function.

4.2. *Socrates' refutation of 4.1*

4.2.1. Socrates argues that if the virtues differ as Protagoras claims, then they cannot resemble each other, but surely we should admit not only that justice is just, but also that piety is just, not only that piety is pious but also that justice is pious? In which case the virtues do resemble each other.

4.2.2. Protagoras accepts the resemblance, but denies it is significant: everything resembles everything else to some degree.

4.2.3. Socrates argues the resemblance is significant: different virtues have the same contrary vice, e.g.

folly is the opposite of wisdom,

it is also the opposite of *sophrosyne*.

Since one thing has one and only one contrary, this implies wisdom and *sophrosyne* are one and the same.

4.3. Socrates asks whether a man can exercise *sophrosyne* in doing wrong.

4.3.1. Protagoras denies that this is possible, but admits many people would say it is. He accepts the job of defending the view of the many against Socrates' questioning, but after a few exchanges the discussion collapses. Protagoras delivers a short speech on the relativity of benefit and consequently of the good and an argument breaks out when Socrates tries to get him to answer briefly.

5. Interlude

The bystanders join in the argument, persuading Socrates and Protagoras to carry on their discussion. Brief speeches by the famous sophists Prodicus and Hippias allow Plato to satirize the pedantic verbal distinctions of the one and the complacent pomposity of the other.

5.1. *Discussion of Simonides' poem*

The discussion reopens with Protagoras questioning Socrates about the meaning of some lines of Simonides. Socrates answers him, and engages in an elaborate analysis of the poem dragging in various other poetic authorities. His exegesis is a satire of standard sophistical ways of dealing with poetry. In the course of his exposition Socrates takes the opportunity to propose ideas which are clearly his own: that the only true misfortune is loss of knowledge (345 b) and that no one willingly does wrong (345 e). He ends by pointing to the futility of the exercise: the poet cannot be questioned, disputes about what he means are inconclusive, far better to argue and dispute with living people, putting their opinions to the test (347 e).

5.2. Protagoras now agrees to answer Socrates' questions.

6. Socrates' questions (cf. 4) reiterated

Are wisdom, *sophrosyne*, courage, justice, and piety five names for the same thing, or are they five distinct parts of virtue?

6.1. *Protagoras' response*

They are five parts: wisdom, *sophrosyne*, justice, and piety resemble each other closely; courage is something quite different. The proof of this is that a man can be ignorant, intemperate, unjust, and impious and yet courageous in the extreme.

6.2. *Socrates' refutation of 6.1*

Socrates questions Protagoras, to win his agreement to the following argument:

> Courage involves boldness.
> Courage is a virtue.
> Virtue is always something fine (noble, honourable).

Relevant knowledge enables men to act boldly.

Bold action based on relevant knowledge is something fine.

Bold action based on ignorance is not something fine, it is mere rashness, not courage.

> Wisdom, then, is courage.

6.3. Protagoras' response to 6.2

Protagoras counters Socrates' argument with an analogy. The

same pattern of argument would allow the inference that wisdom is strength:

> The strong are powerful.
>
> Those who have relevant knowledge (e.g. of martial arts) are more powerful than those who do not, and one who acquires relevant knowledge is more powerful than he was before he acquired it.
>
> From that by analogy with Socrates' argument in 6.2, one could then infer that wisdom is strength.

Protagoras diagnoses the fallacy in Socrates' argument as turning on presuming it is possible to infer from

> 'The courageous are confident' (which Protagoras accepts) to
>
> 'The confident are courageous' (which Protagoras rejects).
>
> (Implicit in his argument is a sense of the distinction between the 'is/are' of class inclusion:
>
> e.g. 'The Muses are deities' = The class of Muses is included in the class of deities and the 'is/are' of class identity:
>
> e.g. 'Divinities are deities' = The class of divinities is identical with the class of deities).

6.4. *Socrates' hedonistic argument for the identity and teachability of the virtues*

Socrates does not challenge Protagoras' analysis of his argument (although it is by no means obvious he is guilty of the fallacy of which he is accused). Instead he constructs a new and rather surprising argument. He first argues for the identification of pleasure with good and of pain with evil. He then considers the common opinion that one can act wrongly when 'overcome by pleasure'. Socrates has already won Protagoras' agreement to the claim that nothing overcomes knowledge: a man who knows what is good will act accordingly. He now argues to the conclusion that even a hedonistic theory of the nature of good and evil leaves us with the conclusion that all wrongdoing proceeds from ignorance. Being 'overcome by pleasure' is failing to measure the relative quantities and qualities of the pleasures and pains brought about by a given act.

He then argues against Protagoras' attempt to separate courage from the other virtues. He characterizes fear as 'expectation of evil', and wins his audience's agreement to the claim that no one willingly goes after the evil he fears. The rash man and the courageous man differ in knowledge, the coward and the courageous man likewise. Cowardice is ignorance of what should be feared, i.e. of what evils are to be expected; courage is knowledge of such things.

Protagoras grudgingly admits defeat.

D.7. *Envoi*

Socrates summarizes the conclusions of the debate, pointing out how he and Protagoras seem to have exchanged positions to some extent. Protagoras offers a courteous reply and suggests they continue the discussion on another occasion, and the dialogue ends.

Here is the summary Socrates gives (361 a) of the outcome of his debate with Protagoras:

What odd beings you are, Socrates and Protagoras. The one of you starts off by asserting virtue cannot be taught and now strives to contradict himself and prove that everything—justice, *sophrosyne*, courage—is knowledge: on which basis virtue would indeed seem thoroughly teachable. But, if virtue be something other than knowledge—as Protagoras attempted to assert—then clearly it will not be teachable: if, however, it does appear that it is in its entirety knowledge, as you argue, Socrates, then it would be astonishing if it cannot be taught. Protagoras, on the other hand, who had claimed it could be taught, now urges the contrary position, and virtue now seems to be well nigh anything at all except knowledge—and that would make it utterly unteachable.

This summary represents no victory as such on the part of either disputant. It represents rather the conclusions which can be drawn from the whole debate:

If virtue is not knowledge, then it cannot be taught.
If virtue is knowledge, it should be teachable.

We are left, in the light of the debates in the rest of the early dialogues, with the puzzle that there seem to be no acceptable and credible candidates to be considered teachers of virtue, and that if, as the real Socrates seems to have held, virtue is knowledge, it is odd that no one seems able to define the various virtues. What kind of knowledge could constitute virtue remains a matter of conjecture.

We are left also with considerable puzzlement about particular moments in the development of the argument of the dialogue. The argument for the identity of wisdom and *sophrosyne*, for example, from their both having folly as their opposite depends on the thoroughly dubious claim that there is only one opposite to anything. The notion of an opposite is not a very clear one; it is none the less a notion of considerable importance in early Greek philosophy. Heraclitus is famous for his belief in the unity of the opposites; there are Pythagorean lists of opposites that look as if they are intended to present ultimate contrasts in terms of which the universe is structured; there is an interesting debate amongst the early philosophers as to whether perception is of like by like or of unlike by unlike that seems to be based on the notion of the opposites. None the less, it is not even clear what kind of notion the notion of opposites is.

'The town hall is opposite the railway station' states a relation of place, 'morning is the opposite of evening' states a temporal relation defined within the diurnal cycle. Some kinds of opposition relations are logical; negation and contradiction are logical forms of opposition, and so presumably is the logical relation of exclusion. If, however, we consider the case of negation, then it does not seem to be true that there is only one negation of any given expression. For example, 'Plato is not a philosopher' and 'It is not the case that Plato is a philosopher' are both negations of 'Plato is a philosopher'; they are clearly not the same expression though they are logically equivalent. Some logicians, but not all, would express their relation to each other by saying they state the same proposition; even so, they are not the same sentence. Even, then, if we concede that there is only one proposition that is the negation of any given proposition, it is not even true that there is only one sentence that is the negation of a given sentence. When we move from the clear relation of negation to the much more plastic notion of opposition, there seems absolutely no reason to accept that there is only one opposite to anything. Aristotle's discussion of virtue provides sufficient evidence to the contrary. He argues that virtues are the mean between two contrary vices. Courage, for example, is the mean between cowardice, a vice of deficiency, and rashness, a vice of excess. If we ask what, in this construction, is the opposite of courage, then rashness and cowardice seem equally reasonable candidates, despite the fact that cowardice might be the answer lying closer at hand. Equally, rashness and cowardice are opposites. What is the opposite of mercy: justice?, strictness?, harshness?, cruelty? It is surely the case that they are all opposites of mercy.

Even in the case of the spatial relation which seems to furnish one of the metaphorical foundations of the concept of opposition it is not the case that there can be only one thing opposite any given thing: the fact that the town hall is opposite the railway station does not exclude the possibility that, for example, the church is also opposite the railway station, without this implying the church and the town hall are one and the same. The nature of any given opposition relation is defined in terms of a particular field of relations, the nature of that field of relations determining whether or not there is indeed only one opposite to any given term in that field.

It is morally certain that Plato was aware of the falsity of Socrates' claim that there is only one opposite to anything. Given that its falsity follows immediately from the existence of ambiguous terms, it is at least possible that being aware of it he has put into Socrates' mouth an argument he knows to be based on a false premiss.

The hedonistic argument that Socrates proposes in the *Protagoras* poses serious problems for an interpreter. The earlier dialogues contain nothing to suggest Socrates is a hedonist; dialogues of Plato's middle period contain vigorously anti-hedonist arguments; the *Philebus*, in the later period, revisits the question of the place of pleasure in human life, and argues to a much more positive, though admittedly not a hedonist, view.

It is possible to interpret the hedonistic argument of the *Protagoras* as evidence of a hedonist stage in the development of Plato's ethical theorizing. Although such an interpretation of the *Protagoras* collides with the prejudices of many Platonists, it is by no means devoid of merit or plausibility; it would explain the extraordinary vehemence of Plato's attack on hedonism in the *Phaedo*, which would then represent Plato's rejection of what he had come to see, no doubt under Pythagorean influence, as a terrible error. It is equally possible that the hedonistic argument is not evidence of Plato's philosophical commitments at the time of the dialogue's composition, or of the views of Socrates at the time of the imagined conversation with Protagoras. It may be that the introduction of the identification of pleasure with the good is intended to give particular force to Socrates' argument against the possibility of people being overcome by pleasure.

It must be admitted that the argument Socrates proposes is not particularly convincing. The belief that no one willingly does wrong, that all wrongdoing is error, is a familiar Socratic paradox. It depends for its plausibility on the prior assumption that all voluntary action is the expression of choice. The common belief that an agent can be overcome by pleasure depends on a quite different assumption, namely that action proceeds not from choice only, but also from impulse. The model Socrates proposes in the *Protagoras* for what it would mean to be overcome by pleasure, to give in to oneself, is that it would consist of acting on the basis of an erroneous belief that a given action will produce greater pleasure than another, when the reverse is actually the case. Since Socrates' fundamental assumptions about the nature of voluntary action are such that any account of acting when overcome by pleasure must be an account of a kind of choice, a decision between one possible course of action and another, then, once the hedonist identification of pleasure with the good has been made, the essential nature of the choice the agent faces in action is which pleasure to choose. In this construction, choosing the greater pleasure is a success, not an example of giving in to oneself; choosing the lesser of two pleasures because one is immersed in and distracted by that particular pleasure is a case of error (one chooses the lesser good having failed to discover the other was the greater). Socrates intends his argument to eliminate the claim that one can act out of weakness of will or overwhelming impulse; all that has really occurred is that he has set up the discussion on the basis of a model of action which excludes, tacitly and a priori, the possibility he appears to be arguing against.

Protagoras' personal claims to teach virtue seem hollow at the end of the dialogue: he can only teach virtue if virtue is knowledge, and if he possesses that knowledge which is the essence of virtue, and Protagoras' relativism excludes him from being able to make a claim to possess that knowledge to any greater degree than anyone who cared to dispute it with him. It would certainly be unsafe for a young man to place his soul in the hands of Protagoras and hope to learn virtue from him.

5

Philosopher and anti-philosopher:
the *rhetor*

Gorgias of Leontini was a famous orator and teacher: he came to
Athens as an ambassador from Leontini in 427 BCE and won
both the admiration of the Assembly for his stylish speeches and
its vote in support of alliance with Leontini against Syracuse.
Gorgias travelled widely and lived to an immense age. He practised and taught a rich and elevated style of oratory ornamented
with a mannered poetical vocabulary and a constant flow of
figures of speech. Surprisingly, he was an accomplished im-
promptu orator, fully capable of sustaining his heightened style
when speaking without a prepared text. Like other exponents of
the arts of oratory he specialized in set-piece exhibitions of his
skill. He wrote and published several of his speeches, the style of
which had a powerful influence on his contemporaries, though it
later fell into disfavour.

Amongst Gorgias' pupils and followers were the Meno who is a
principal speaker in the Platonic dialogue named after him and
the speech-writer and teacher Isocrates, a slightly older contemporary of Plato, and the founder of an institute of higher
learning, the base curriculum of which was grounded on the
transmission of received ethical values and the practical and academic study of literature. Gorgias himself does not seem to have
claimed to be a teacher of virtue: he taught the skills of rhetoric,
developing in his students the ability to persuade and convince an
audience, and encouraging them to acquire a capacity for which
he himself was famous, namely the ability to respond to an audience's questions with confidence and self-possession. He seems
to have taught his pupils by means of having them learn speeches
by heart, as well as by offering them tips and advice on how to
influence an audience. He appears in the *Gorgias* together with
Polus, a younger orator and writer, and Callicles, his host in

Athens, a young and ambitious aristocrat, as the representative of the educational claims and pretensions of rhetoric.

Gorgias is presented as claiming to teach

The power to convince by means of speech the jurymen in a lawcourt, the Council in their Chamber, the members in the Assembly, those present at any civic gathering. With this power the doctor and the trainer will be your slaves, the business man will end up making money . . . for you, able as you are to speak and convince the masses (452 e).

He offers training in rhetoric as the high road to power and influence. Such a prospectus could hardly fail to gain clients in the Athens of his day or of Plato's.

Socrates presses Gorgias to clarify what exactly rhetoric is: he points out that the ability to persuade is not the exclusive province of the *rhetor*, the teacher too seeks to persuade. He asks Gorgias (454 a) 'of what kind of persuasion is rhetoric the craft, and persuasion about what?' Gorgias answers him: 'Of that kind of persuasion which occurs in lawcourts and other mobs, as I said earlier, and about what things are just and what unjust.'

Socrates now makes a sharp contrast between two ways in which we may be persuaded of something: in the one case we may come to know something is true because we have learned it, in the other we may be persuaded to believe something is true.

The distinction Socrates makes is an important one, but not a simple one. The statement 'G believes that p is true' does not entail that p is indeed true; however, the statement 'G knows that p is true' does entail that p is true. It is possible to believe a false proposition is true, but it is not possible to know one is true; it is, of course, possible to believe that one knows a proposition when the proposition is not in fact true. 'G knows that p is true' entails that p is true, but 'G asserts that he knows that p is true' does not entail that p is true. Knowledge may be infallible; claims to knowledge are not.

The crucial point of Socrates' distinction becomes visible when he presses Gorgias as to which of the two forms of persuasion rhetoric is: 'Shall we, then, establish two forms of persuasion, the one producing belief without knowledge, the other, knowledge?'

'Certainly.'

'So which of these two kinds of persuasion about just and unjust things does rhetoric effect in the lawcourt or the other mobs, that which produces belief without knowledge, or that which produces knowledge?'

'Well, evidently that from which belief comes.'

'Then it seems that rhetoric is the author of the persuasion which leads to belief, but which does not teach about the just and the unjust.'

It is not the architects who brought about the building of the city walls of Athens; Themistocles and Pericles did that by means of their ability to sway the Assembly. The orator, Gorgias argues, is a man of great power; he possesses a skill in verbal combat which means that the practitioner of other crafts cannot stand against him if they are in competition to win support in the Assembly. His competitive skill can, of course, be used for good or evil, as Gorgias readily admits. The same is true of any fighting skill. And just as we should not blame the martial arts or the instructors who teach them for the misconduct of a trained fighter who attacked his parents, so we should not blame the art of rhetoric or the *rhetor* who teaches it for the faults of an orator who uses his skills to an unjust purpose.

The *rhetor* can convince people, provided, of course, they are not expert in the matters under discussion. Rhetoric works with the ignorant. For the *rhetor* to be effective in persuading us of something, it is not necessary that he should have expert knowledge of the subject; what he needs is to possess the ability to speak powerfully and persuasively in such a way as to seem to know what he is talking about.

In response to Polus' questioning, Socrates lays aside the courteous restraint he has shown debating with Gorgias, and states bluntly what he thinks of rhetoric. It is not an art or craft (*techne*) at all. It is merely a knack. He compares it to cookery, which, he says, is a kind of imitation of the art of medicine, being in itself no more than a knack of titillating and pleasing, a part of the practice of flattery.

'According to my account rhetoric is a spurious image of a part of politics.'

'What? Then do you hold it is something fine or something base?'

'For myself, base, for I call evil things base.' (463 d)

Socrates builds an analogy: two arts serve our bodily welfare, the art of gymnastics keeps us in good health, the art of medicine furnishes a corrective to restore health when we are ill; cosmetics is the spurious image of gymnastics (it is a practice which gives the appearance of health), and cookery is a spurious image of the art of medicine (instead of providing what our bodies need to restore health, cookery titillates and gratifies our appetites and tastes). Two arts serve the needs of our souls, legislation and justice; sophistry is the fake image of legislation, rhetoric the fake image of justice. The spurious images draw their power from people's ignorance.

Socrates stands over against Gorgias as the teacher-friend who uses the discipline of systematic questioning to lead his associates from ill-founded assumptions to acknowledged ignorance which can then become the starting-point for learning; Gorgias, as a *rhetor* and teacher of rhetoric, is made to appear as an exploiter of ignorance and unquestioned prejudice. However gentle the portrait of Gorgias himself, there is no doubt Plato is calling him to account for the arrogance and the selfishness of his associates Polus and Callicles. Their hard-edged styles of argument, their contempt for the sober, reflective, self-critical philosophical ideal Socrates is made to embody, their devotion to power as a value and to the ability to control the actions of others as an end all flow directly from the values implicit in Gorgias' position.

The dialogue throws into sharp relief opposed and irreconcilable ideals of life. Plato presents the philosophical ideal of life as a rigorous quest for truth: the philosopher seeks to know reality; he rejoices in the discovery of his own ignorance, since ignorance is better than error and delusion, and acknowledged ignorance the starting point of learning; he fears nothing save the loss of knowledge; the possession of knowledge is the sole key to excellence since knowledge and virtue are one; he values the guidance and instruction of sound law, and, if in error he does wrong, sees punishment as a form of therapy, preferring punishment to the danger of his wrongdoing going uncorrected. Callicles derides Socrates' devotion to philosophy. Philosophy, he says, is good for boys; a grown man should put aside such childish things for more adult pursuits, public affairs and self-advancement in civic life. The superior man liberates himself from the constrictions of the law, a mere array of conventions, which, in a democratic society, restrict his freedom of action in the interests of the many; he follows instead the law of nature, seeking happiness in the fulfilment of his wants and needs. He is not satisfied with a merely equal share of the good things available; he, rightly in his own eyes, seeks the greater share he merits by nature, and which more adequately serves to promote his happiness.

The contrast Callicles makes between nature (*physis*) and convention (*nomos*) reflects a familiar and significant theme in the intellectual debates of the sophists and of their period, a theme which has a sharply political aspect. Philosophical investigations into the ultimate ground of human values and social and political structures furnished ready-made ideological weapons which the various political factions and interest groups were keen to use against each other. As Callicles' arguments here, and those of Thrasymachus in the *Republic* well illustrate, the claims of nature could be advanced as an ideological underpinning for an ethic of power-seeking egoism, an ethic which frequently attempted to portray itself as the classic aristocratic value-system, and which in reality embodied the aspirations of an oligarchic mentality with a crystalline awareness of its own class interest. The claims of *nomos*, by contrast, tended to be associated with the more egalitarian ideological position of democratic political thinkers (egalitarian, of course, within the limits of classical Greek democratic thinking), which concerned itself with the liberties and interests of a citizenry whose freedom and whose rights were always and inevitably foregrounded against the contrasting lack of rights and freedom of an enormous slave population and the limited privileges conceded to resident aliens. It is not, however, possible to line up *physis* and *nomos* thinkers into two groups the members of each of which share homogeneous ethical and political outlooks. Protagoras, for example, made an extensive use of the concept of convention, taking it far beyond the limits of the philosophical interpretation of human and social values and arguing that it is by convention that things possess even the sensuous qualities we attribute to them.

The ultimate ground of values and of value concepts is not by any means fully explored in the *Gorgias*, and the fact that here, as in his confrontation with Thrasymachus in the *Republic*, Socrates appears as the opponent of a partisan of *physis* should not lead to the simplistic conclusion that Socrates therefore accepts *nomos* as the sufficient ground of values. In the *Protagoras* he stands equally opposed to the foremost proponent of the *nomos* approach.

The ideal of life for which Callicles and Polus both argue is that of the tyrant, the man who by his own abilities can take and hold power, finding his happiness in the satisfaction of his own needs and desires, and enforcing his will on others while being at no risk from them. Socrates regards such a man as meriting pity rather than admiration: for him the point is not to find fulfilment in a life where one has the freedom and the power to do exactly what one desires; it is necessary first to find out what it is worthwhile desiring. He even argues (466 e) that if, as Polus thinks, power is good, then the person who is able to do absolutely what he chooses may, in a serious and important sense, reasonably be called powerless: 'For I assert, Polus, that the *rhetor* and the tyrant have the least power in the *polis*: . . . they do virtually nothing they want, they do whatever it is they think best.' A freedom that licenses injustice is, for Socrates, a disabling freedom. To act unjustly, he claims, is a worse thing than to suffer injustice. Education and upright conduct are the source of happiness; injustice injures its perpetrator worse than its victim; the worst thing that can happen is to act unjustly and escape the punishment which one needs as corrective and cure. An ill-educated tyrant would, then, be a most unfortunate being, licensed by his position to act in any way he chooses, and so powerful as to be above all fear of punishment: for Socrates he is at the scant mercy of his own ignorance.

The *rhetor*, the sophist, and the tyrant emerge in the *Gorgias* as the three icons of the anti-philosopher.

The philosopher's resolute and self-critical search for truth may find its fruition in the possession of genuine and testable knowledge of human, social, and political values; and at the least, the application of the method of systematic questioning by Socrates, Plato's canonical image of the ideal philosopher, shows how error, delusion, and ill-grounded opinion can be purged by therapeutic destruction-testing, leaving the mind awakened to its own ignorance and opened to enquiry.

The sophist, even so great a sophist as Protagoras, does not possess the knowledge that would validate his claims to offer an education in excellence; he is even unaware, for Plato, of the degree to which all he has to offer is ungrounded opinion, mere guesses at the truth unsustained by any sound method, even though that method lies at hand in the question-battle technique his pupils learn. The lamentable result of the sophist's educational programme is brought to life in Euthydemus, a person skilled in the rituals of formal verbal combat, and well capable of impressing a naïve audience with his ability to refute and embarrass an adversary, but possessed himself of no true knowledge, and, given the self-satisfaction he derives from his success in defeating others, utterly unmotivated to seek it. At best Plato's sophist is a sad figure, selling the empty appearances of a knowledge he does not possess, a quack unaware of his own quackery; at worst he is a profoundly sinister figure corroding the body politic with his convenient but ungrounded theories and the argumentative agility he purveys as civic virtue.

The *rhetor* is presented as meriting equal contempt. To practise and teach the skills of persuasion with no regard to the truth, the use of those skills to subvert the operation of the Assembly and the court of justice to one's own ends is, for Plato, the very antithesis of the philosopher's political and social duty. Plato follows the historical Socrates in arguing that political decisions should be based on expert knowledge, not left to the vagaries of the vote. The *Crito*, in which Socrates, in prison and under sentence of death, refuses to co-operate with the escape plan his friend Crito has arranged, constitutes, in major part, an argument that there is a civic duty to submit to the workings of the law, an argument which gains power and force in Socrates' mouth, since he is while arguing awaiting the execution on his own person of an unjust and unreasonable sentence passed on the basis of a false verdict by an unjust court. The Socrates of the *Crito* and the *Phaedo*, obedient to the law even when it treats him unjustly, and happy in the face of a death he freely accepts, presents a model of the philosopher's political and social duty that is utterly irreconcilable with and diametrically opposed to the image of the self-interested persuader of courts and avoider of punishment which Polus presents as his ideal in the *Gorgias*.

The sophist is presented as the antithesis of the philosopher as educator and theorist, the *rhetor* his antithesis as citizen in the Assembly and the courts: the tyrant, whom Polus and Callicles canvass as image of the ideal life, Plato presents as the most perfect icon of the anti-philosopher. The tyrant, as Polus and Callicles present him, is the man whose position of power allows him to act exactly as he chooses, to enforce his will on others and to escape the punishment and the retribution his acts might receive if he were merely a private citizen. Callicles develops the portrait in direct contrast to what Socrates says (491 d) is the common view, that one should be 'moderate, master of himself, in control of his own pleasures and desires'. According to Callicles, the fine thing according to nature is that one should develop one's appetites and desires without restraint and acquire the power to satisfy them. Moderation and self-control are alien to the naturally superior man. The notion that there is something shameful in a lack of restraint is humbug. Here we see two fundamentally opposed ideals: the tyrant seeks to rule others so as to seek his own happiness in serving his own desires and appetites, free from fear of punishment or retribution; the philosopher seeks to attain self-mastery and to acquire knowledge, which, if he attains it, will, in Plato's view, equip him to serve his fellows as a true educator and the State as a source of sound advice; indeed, he would be uniquely equipped to exercise the political power the tyrant misuses to his own ends.

In so far as the *Gorgias* is to some extent at least a pamphlet against any claims on the part of *rhetors* to furnish an education for citizenship, it must be conceded that to the degree that the conception of education at issue is that proposed by Gorgias the case Socrates advances would be difficult to rebut. In so far, however, as the arguments of the dialogue are directed at demonstrating that rhetoric as such is devoid of value, they carry less conviction. Indeed, Plato returns to the discussion of rhetoric in the *Phaedrus* and seems to modify his position quite considerably, emphasizing the need for the *rhetor* to possess a sound knowledge of the object-matter of his discourse if he is not to make himself ridiculous; he even needs knowledge in order to deceive his hearers effectively. The power of rhetoric, Socrates argues, is greater in matters about which people are in disagreement; in matters of common agreement the power of rhetoric is the less. Equally we find in the *Phaedrus* indications that the *rhetor* needs to possess knowledge of how to construct a discourse, 'just like a living thing with its own body' (264 c), so that it is ordered, shaped, and formed in such a way that all its parts stand in an appropriate relation to each other and to the discourse as a whole.

In the *Phaedrus*, that is to say, the arguments Plato has Socrates advance suggest that, despite what he has said in the *Gorgias*, there can be an art (*techne*) of rhetoric. They seem even to lead to the startling conclusion that if the *rhetor* wishes to teach his art, then that is possible, but in order to do so he needs to be a philosopher: he needs to understand human psychology and to be able to relate the various kinds of discourse to the various personality types susceptible to persuasion by the different forms of speech; he needs to know the truth about the matters on which orators habitually speak, the nature of justice, goodness, and beauty, the nature of political values. A speaker or writer possessing such knowledge merits, says Socrates, to be called a philosopher.

Until a man knows the truth about each matter on which he speaks or writes, becomes capable of defining everything individually and, having defined things, knows how to divide them up into classes until no further division is possible, and understands likewise the nature of the soul, discerning the modes of discourse suited to different natures, organizing and ornamenting what he says in such a way as to address complex and elegantly structured speeches to complex souls and simple ones to simple souls—until he has achieved all this he will not possess the ability to exploit the art of speaking (in so far as it is in the nature of utterances to be governed by an art) whether in order to teach or in order to persuade . . . (*Phdr.* 277 b–c)

Aristotle's *Rhetoric* carries the suggestions of Socrates' argument in the *Phaedrus* to their conclusion, presenting itself as a technical manual of the art of rhetoric, teaching how to persuade one's hearers of the truth by means of speeches and arguments constructed and presented with a skill based on a sound understanding of human psychology.

6

Learning and recollection: the *Meno*

A significant turning-point in the development of Plato's thought was his encounter with the living tradition of Pythagorean philosophy. During his visits to Syracuse Plato made the acquaintance of Archytas of Tarentum, a distinguished representative of the Pythagorean school. Archytas was a skilled mathematician interested in the mathematical analysis of the nature of music. He was also an important political figure in his own city. His friendship must have been an important factor in developing Plato's interest in Pythagorean philosophy. The influence of Pythagorean thought on Plato is beyond doubt: apart from the immediate evidence of numerous passages in the dialogues, we have the explicit testimony of Aristotle.

The transforming influence of Pythagoreanism is clearly evident in the *Meno*. This dialogue takes up once again the question of the teachability of virtue. Meno opens the dialogue (70 a) with a question: 'Can you tell me, Socrates, whether virtue can be taught, or is it something not taught but acquired by practice? Or is it neither something practised nor something learned but comes to exist in men by nature or in some other way?'

The patterns of argument, and the contents of the arguments in the opening pages of the dialogue, are familiar. Meno initially defends the view that virtue is one thing for a man ('to be equal to the task of dealing with civic affairs, and to do so in such a way as to benefit his friends and to harm his enemies taking care to avoid harm himself') and another thing for a woman ('good housekeeping, safeguarding domestic property, and obedience to her husband'), one thing for boys, another for girls, one thing for free men, another for slaves. Socrates quickly undermines this attempt. He asks what is the *eidos*, the form or character, shared by all the different kinds of virtue, which makes virtue virtue. After some discussion Meno identifies this basic character of virtue as 'capacity to govern human beings'. This attempt at definition is brought to nothing. Socrates constructs scientific analogies to make clear what kind of formula a definition is, one showing how a plurality is held together in unity. Meno attempts a second definition: virtue is 'desire for fine things and the ability to acquire them'. This definition too is subjected to Socrates' customary pattern of questioning, and it too collapses.

Before I met you, Socrates, I heard that you are a thoroughly bewildered person who makes others bewildered as well. And, indeed, I now find you simply enchanting me with spells and witchery so that I am reduced to bewilderment myself. If I am permitted the levity, I must compare you, because of your appearance and for other reasons, to the sting-ray; if anyone approaches it and touches it, it numbs him—and that is more or less what you have done to me. I truly feel my mind and my mouth are numb: I have no answer to give you. And I have held forth on innumerable occasions and at length to sizeable audiences on the subject of virtue—and done it well, or so I thought! And now I cannot even say what it is. (80 a–b)

Socrates answers:

If the sting-ray is numb itself when it induces numbness in others, then for my own part I accept the likeness: if it isn't, then I don't. It is not that I possess certainty myself and so reduce others to bewilderment—on the contrary it is because I am the worst possible case of bewilderment that I induce bewilderment in others.

Now that he and Meno are in the same state of bewildered ignorance, Socrates offers to continue their shared investigation into the nature of virtue. Meno raises a question of great importance:

And how are you going to search for something, Socrates, when you have no idea whatsoever what it is? What kind of unknown somewhat will you propose as the object of your search? And if you are lucky enough to come across it, how will you know it is that unknown somewhat? (80 d)

Meno is proposing a classic sophistic conundrum: it is impossible to enquire into what one knows, since one knows it and there is no point in the enquiry, nor into what one does not know, since then one cannot know what the object of the enquiry is to be.

The conundrum points to a philosophical problem which requires a serious answer. A question cannot be asked from a position of utter ignorance. A question is not the expression of an open-ended and formless curiosity; it expresses ignorance, but at the same time specifies that ignorance against a backcloth of explicit or implicit knowledge or belief which gives form and significance to the ignorance the question expresses. The questioner expects to be able to recognize whether or not any given formula is an answer to the specific question she or he has posed: not only whether or not it happens to be the correct answer, but whether it can count as an answer at all. If questioning expressed mere ignorance, there would be no criteria available to determine what might count as an answer. The act of questioning presupposes the possession of knowledge or belief: in questioning the questioner discloses not only the ignorance which his question expresses but also the knowledge or belief which allows him to diagnose his own ignorance and to formulate his question.

Socrates' answer lifts the whole discussion to a different plane: he offers on the authority of 'wise men and women, . . . certain priests and priestesses' an account of the immortality of the soul and of its reincarnation which is almost certainly Pythagorean in origin.

They say the human soul is immortal: at one moment it comes to an end, what is called dying, at another it comes to rebirth, but it is never subject to annihilation . . . and so, since the soul is immortal and has been born many times, and has seen everything there is, both here and in Hades, there is nothing it has not learned. It is no wonder, then, that it has the capacity to recollect all that it formerly knew about virtue and so forth. All nature is akin: the soul has learned all things: there is no reason, then, why by recollecting one single thing—having learned it, as men say—it should not be enabled to find out everything else, provided the enquiry be conducted in a resolute and tenacious manner. Enquiry and learning are entirely recollection. (81 c–d)

To convince Meno this is not merely a pious fable, Socrates now carries out a curious experiment: he subjects Meno's young slave to a series of questions about a simple geometrical figure as a result of which the boy, though he has no knowledge of mathematics, is able to solve a mathematical problem.

In the first stages of Socrates' dialogue with him, the boy confidently propounds opinions which are subjected to testing by Socrates in his customary fashion. The boy comes to recognize he is mistaken, and becomes bewildered. 'Do you think he would have tried to search and learn what he thought he already knew though he did not know it,' Socrates asks Meno (84 c), 'until he had been reduced to a state of bewilderment, recognizing his lack of knowledge, and thirsting to know?'

Socrates continues questioning in such a manner as to draw the boy's attention to particular features of the figure they are considering, so that the boy comes to recognize the simple basic mathematical relationships which enable him to solve the problem. Given that the boy has, as Socrates says, been motivated by discovering he is ignorant and by his bewilderment to search earnestly for the truth, then Socrates' method seems to be an effective means of enabling him to learn: his attention is drawn to aspects of the geometrical figure which concretely embody the relationships he needs to know in order to solve the problem. As his attention is focused on the relevant aspects of the figure, Socrates questions him in such a way as to open up the possibility of his recognizing the mathematical relationships relating the various parts of the figure. At this point the boy is enabled to form true opinions as to the relations. 'Just now these opinions are freshly activated—dreamlike. But as someone keeps on posing him these same questions in a variety of different ways, you can see that eventually his knowledge concerning these matters will be as exact as anyone's.'

Later passages in the dialogue make this final stage clearer: what is required is that he reasons out the ground of things being as they are, then his true belief will become knowledge. The pattern of his learning is like this:

(*a*) False opinion subjected to effective questioning leads to the refutation of the false opinion.

(*b*) Refutation leads to ignorance and bewilderment.

(*c*) Ignorance and bewilderment lead to a thirst for knowledge.

(*d*) A thirst for knowledge leads to a resolute and persistent enquiry.

(*e*) Resolute and persistent enquiry leads to true opinion.

(*f*) Continual questioning of the ground of one's true opinions leads to knowledge.

This pattern of learning, moving from false opinion confidently held through bewildered ignorance to correct opinions and finally to knowledge marks a transition-point in the development of Plato's understanding of method. The earlier dialogues have demonstrated the power of systematic questioning, when used as Socrates does in his dialectical arguments with intellectual seriousness and when directly addressed to the opinions proposed by an interlocutor, to test the consistency and coherence of those opinions. We here see acted out in Socrates' questioning of the slave-boy an application of the method of systematic questioning directed not merely as before at the consistency-testing of opinions, but now moving on from that to uncovering the truth; not merely at removing erroneous views and letting an interlocutor recognize his own ignorance, but now using the recognition of ignorance and the motivating power of bewilderment to enable the interlocutor to discern the truth and to acquire true belief.

It is important to recognize that the experiment involves no transmission of information from teacher to learner. In the experiment carried out by Socrates, an educative process has gone on: the boy has been enabled to learn and led to learn, but he has not been offered information or instruction.

It is frequently objected that the experiment is devoid of value since Socrates has carried the boy with him by means of leading questions. The objection is beside the point: leading questions are still questions. It is still the boy who makes the crucial series of judgements on which the mathematical argument depends. He is free at any point to dissent from the step in the inference sequence that Socrates proposes to him. Each step in turn is presented to the boy for his acceptance or rejection. At each stage it is the judgement the boy makes that moves the argument on. Indeed, it might well be argued that the experiment does not ultimately depend for its power on the use of the question form: even if Socrates had proposed to the boy a series of true statements about the geometrical relations actually existing amongst the various parts of the figure under discussion rather than asking him questions, unless the slave-boy is to be thought of as simply believing whatever Socrates asserts merely because he asserts it, then he must be supposed to discern in some manner that what he has been told is true. What Plato is trying to establish is not merely that the slave-boy has been enabled to recollect the truth by means of Socrates' questions, but a more fundamental proposition, that all learning is a matter of recollection.

Plato interprets the experiment and the pattern of learning it discloses as evidence that all we call learning is in reality recollection of knowledge the soul has acquired in earlier existences. It is possible, however, to take the experiment seriously and to conclude as Socrates does that the boy has learned without being instructed, without having recourse to metaphysically expensive theories of reincarnation and recollection as an explanatory framework to make sense of what has happened. Indeed, there is something paradoxical about Plato's approach. He demonstrates in the experiment that once the boy subjects his opinions to the disciplined questioning of Socrates, he becomes capable of actualizing his capacities for active learning. At this point, however, Plato still carries with him a basically passive model of knowledge as the perception of reality. As a result, Plato places very little emphasis on the boy's activity when he interprets the significance of the experiment. Instead he accounts for the boy's developing understanding of the mathematical problem by inferring he must already possess the knowledge he seems at each new stage to demonstrate. There is considerable difference between the recollection of innate but forgotten knowledge and the activation of innate capacities: the conclusion that the boy must have possessed the knowledge necessary to solve the problem, although he was unaware that he possessed it, is as unsatisfactory as it is unnecessary.

An alternative interpretation of the experiment might emphasize the cognitive activity of the boy, focusing on him and what he does, especially in the second period of questioning when he has been motivated by the realization of his own ignorance. It would see Socrates' pointing to different parts of the figure and questioning about the mathematical relations embodied in those parts as liberating the boy's innate capacities to recognize similarities and differences, to make simple inferences, and to synthesize, so that he is able to construct for himself an adequate and correct answer to the problem Socrates poses.

Although the theory of recollection and the pattern of learning by which recollection becomes possible are the central focus of the *Meno*, the dialogue opens with the discussion of the teachability of virtue, and it is to this topic that Plato returns in the latter part of the dialogue. The answer now presented is that virtue has no teachers, the pretensions of sophists to teach virtue are vain, virtue is unteachable, and therefore not knowledge. None the less, virtue is clearly exhibited by certain men in public life, some of whose sons are as notable for their lack of it as their fathers are eminent for its practice. It is not, then, simply a matter of natural endowment or genetic inheritance: if it were natural, it could not be acquired as it clearly is; if it were a matter of heredity, virtuous fathers would have virtuous sons. Virtue, Socrates concludes, is a matter of correct opinion: the statesman who excels in conduct of public affairs is like the seer who excels in prediction. Virtue is a divine gift of correct opinion.

How seriously we are to take the conclusions of the *Meno* on the nature of virtue may be doubted. There is too close a reminiscence of the *Ion* in the latter pages of the *Meno* for it to be taken unsalted. Plato was quite happy to allow divine inspiration to poets and rhapsodes, but the point of that was to demolish their claims to be considered seriously as possessors or teachers of knowledge. For Plato to say someone is divinely inspired is an ambiguous compliment: it seems on occasion a polite way of saying the person's achievements may appear impressive but that he himself acts without any real knowledge of what he is doing. In such a case, divine inspiration demythologized is serendipity.

Curiously, Plato also makes another sharply contrasting use of claims to inspiration; when it is Socrates who claims it, as in the *Phaedrus*, or when he quotes priests or priestesses it is Plato's way of surrounding some of his most important and significant philosophical teachings with an aura of religious significance. Any passage in the dialogues which appeals to divine inspiration needs the most careful interpretation. The general pattern seems to be that when Socrates explains the achievements of others as due to divine inspiration, he is denying they are the result of skill, wisdom, or knowledge: when Socrates himself claims divine inspiration or a religious source for his teachings, he is adding religious emphasis to doctrine seriously propounded, but unsupported (in Plato's text at least) by adequate argument to substantiate it.

The *Meno* represents an unstable moment in the development of Plato's ideas. The ungainly structure of the dialogue is evidence of this. The answer given to the questions as to the nature and teachability of virtue is unconvincing and unsatisfying. The theory of recollection represents an interesting and radical attempt to solve the fundamental problems of epistemology, but it solves them at an enormous price, the acceptance of the whole Pythagorean doctrine of the immortality of the soul and of successive rebirth; and even at that far from inconsiderable cost, it still does not explain how in its supposed prenatal existence the soul came to possess the knowledge it recollects in this life. The central philosophical question the dialogue raises is that of how learning occurs, how the learner recognizes or discerns that a given proposition is true. The answer he offers, that learning is a matter of recollecting what we already know but have forgotten, is hopelessly unsatisfactory since the question must be asked about the original acquisition of the knowledge we have come to possess. In effect, all Plato has done is to relocate the problematic moment, to throw it backwards in the learner's biography from the learner's learning in the present moment (which has at least the advantage of being accessible to empirical investigation and conceivably even to experimentation), to a pre-natal existence proposed to us not in virtue of a sequence of rational arguments, but on the unexamined authority of the 'priests and priestesses' under whose guise we may reasonably guess him to conceal the teachings of the Pythagoreans. Moreover, at this point no account is offered of the nature of the objects of knowledge. Given the central importance of mathematics in Pythagorean philosophy, it is interesting that the example Plato presents uses mathematical reasoning, and that it depends on Pythagoras' Theorem for its formal solution. But no conclusion is drawn as to the relative knowability of mathematical truths in comparison with any others. What, however, we may certainly conclude from the nature of the experiment is that Plato is asserting that the truths of mathematics are part of the knowledge gained in earlier existences and capable of recollection in this life.

The dialogue offers no suggestion as to how we are supposed to go about recovering the knowledge we have lost. Socrates' questioning has enabled the slave-boy to recollect a sequence of mathematical truths; there is nothing to suggest how or why he would ever have come to recover the knowledge he had lost in the absence of that questioning.

The *Meno* points beyond itself; it represents a stage in Plato's philosophical activity where the tentative theoretical constructions he has been able to present raise more questions than they answer. It provides powerful evidence against any attempt to generate a static interpretation of Plato, and marks a transition from one major stage in his philosophical investigations to another.

7

Preparing the soul for death: the *Phaedo*

The *Phaedo* purports to recount the conversation between Socrates and his friends in the death cell during the last hours of his life. Commentators of the status of Burnet and Taylor argued fiercely that it is inconceivable that Plato could in any way deviate from the truth in his depiction of the death of Socrates. Their argument was anachronistic: there is plenty of evidence that an imaginative treatment of solemn occasions was thoroughly acceptable in the literary conventions of Plato's day. Moreover, Plato is careful to indicate to the reader that he himself was absent from the scene. The literary aim and function of the dialogue is not simply the recording of how Socrates died. No doubt the dialogue does convey well the atmosphere of Socrates' death cell: his wife in a state of uncontrollable grief, his friends and disciples gathered to share his last moments, the Master himself, dignified and serene, arguing with them about the ultimate question of life and death. The detail of the conversation is another matter. Socrates was a profoundly religious man, and there is no reason to believe he did not accept the belief in immortality for which Plato's Socrates argues, but there is no need to attribute to him the array of arguments with which Plato's Socrates attempts to establish that belief. Equally, Socrates certainly sought for universal definitions, and formulated questions about the ultimate nature of virtue, beauty, and so forth. He may well have asked on occasions 'What is the *eidos* [form, shape] of beauty itself?' or 'What is the *idea* [form, pattern, style, idea] of virtue?', but there is the best of evidence in Aristotle's account of his thought that Socrates never held that the *eidos* or *idea* was a transcendent reality as Plato's Socrates argues in the *Phaedo*.

The setting of the *Phaedo* is important. The dialogue is not merely biography or history, but the setting lends immense weight to the arguments the dialogue contains. Socrates' dying testimony underwrites the philosophical theories Plato presents in this dialogue. There is no greater emphasis Plato could give to the arguments presented in the *Phaedo* than that which the setting in the death cell of Socrates provides. In the dialogue, Socrates moves from his customary role as questioner and on several occasions speaks at length, arguing for views which, whatever the degree of approval with which the historical Socrates might have viewed them, certainly represent a stage in Plato's philosophical development which marks an advance on the positions presented in the *Meno*. Plato uses the speeches of Socrates immediately before his execution in order to lay definitive claim to the Socratic succession: it is Plato's doctrine that Socrates is made to hand down as his ultimate philosophical bequest.

The discussions of the *Phaedo* focus on the general theme of death. Socrates sends a surprising message to the philosopher Evenus:

'Tell him if he is wise to follow after me as quickly as possible. I seem to be taking my departure today, so Athens has decided.'

'What sort of advice is that for Evenus, Socrates?!' said Simmias. 'I have had plenty of dealings with that man, and I hardly imagine he will follow your advice from what I know of him!'

'Indeed,' he said, 'but surely Evenus is a philosopher?'

'Yes', said Simmias.

'Well then, Evenus should be willing—as indeed should every man who takes a worthwhile part in philosophical activity. He won't kill himself, of course; that is said to be forbidden.' (61 c)

After a brief discussion of why it is that suicide is forbidden, Socrates begins to explain (64 a) why it is that a philosopher should look forward to death: 'Other people don't seem to realize that those who pursue philosophy in the right way are actually working at readying themselves for dying and for being dead.'

The true philosopher, Socrates declares, strives to free himself from subjection to the pleasures of the flesh. He strives to separate soul from body: to purify his mind from the distorting influences of pleasure and pain, for if reality and truth are to be known it can only be by pure thought. The philosopher seeks

knowledge of absolute truth, absolute beauty, absolute goodness. These are not to be found in the world of sense experience;
the philosopher must seek them by pure reason unhindered by the
senses. From this it follows that the body is an obstacle to philosophy: the body's needs and its weakness distract us, pleasure
and pain exercise an obsessive influence on us which distorts our
perception of reality. The philosopher needs continually to avoid
any unnecessary involvement in the things of the body in order to
attain the degree of purification (*katharsis*) necessary to enable
him to come to a knowledge of the truth.

'When does the soul attain to truth? When it undertakes an investigation in such a way as to involve the body, it is manifestly led into error
by it.'

'What you say is true.'

'It is by thinking, then, if at all, that it obtains a clear view of reality?'

'Yes.'

'And it thinks best when it is free from such distractions as hearing,
sight, pain, or pleasure, says farewell to the body and, in so far as
possible, becomes separated off, avoiding in so far as it can all contact,
all association with the body as it reaches forth to reality.'

The body is an obstacle to the attainment of knowledge. It is
more than that: it is the root of all evil.

'All this', he said, 'must cause serious philosophers to come to an
opinion they would state as follows: "Here there seems to be a short cut
which leads us to the following conclusion in our intellectual search, that
so long as we possess a body and our soul is contaminated with this kind
of evil, we shall never attain fully the object of our desire—and that
object is the truth. The body's need for nourishment involves us in end-
less troubles. It falls ill, and that proves an obstacle in our quest for
reality. The body fills us with desires, inclinations, fears, every kind of
fancy and folly, with the result that it effectively terminates all our
thinking about anything. The body and the body's desires are the cause
of wars, insurrections, and battles: all wars are started to gain wealth; it
is the body which compels us to the quest for wealth; we are slaves in its
service. Engulfed in such troubles we have not time for philosophy.
Worst of all, if we should happen to obtain leisure enough to engage in
some pattern of enquiry, the body is forever breaking in upon our
search, disturbing us with noisy distractions, preventing our obtaining
clear sight of the truth. Indeed, we see clearly that if we are to have clear

knowledge of anything we must be liberated from the body and contemplate things with the soul alone.'' ' (66 b–d)

The conclusion one might draw from this argument, which must have seemed as extraordinary to Plato's contemporaries as it does to a modern reader, is, as Socrates points out, that there is no hope of our attaining to knowledge of anything until we are liberated from the body by death. So long as we live, if we are serious seekers for truth, we must engage in a determined process of purification (*katharsis*) from all involvement with the body. This notion of *katharsis* is based on Pythagorean ideas. The Pythagorean school practised purification of the body by medicine and of the soul by 'music' (*mousike*) so as to attain to the contemplation of the ultimate order of things. Earlier in the *Phaedo* Socrates has already spoken of his being called by a divine voice to the practice of music, and of his interpretation of this to refer to philosophy 'since philosophy is the supreme music'. The word 'music' here has an extremely broad meaning; it refers to all the arts falling in the sphere of the Muses. Socrates, as a philosopher, has prepared himself for death, since he has long practised the purification of the soul by removing it as far as possible from contamination by the body. Death comes to him as the culmination of his philosophical practice of self-purification: 'Why, then, as I said in the beginning, it would be ridiculous for a man who has spent all his life training himself to live in a state as near to death as he can, to become disturbed at the approach of death.'

Philosophy for the Socrates of the *Phaedo* is a systematic self-liberation from the beguiling influences of pleasure and pain which give to sense-experience an intensity and vividness that delude us into taking mere sensuous appearances for reality. It is this ability of the philosopher to purify his mind from contamination by bodily concerns that makes him truly virtuous. He becomes capable of true courage and true *sophrosyne* since he has transcended the fear of death and has freed himself from attachment to physical things. Liberated from the obsessive and deluding power of pleasure and pain, the philosopher can face the world as he knows it to be, freed from the desires and fears in which most of humanity are trapped. For other men, the semblance of virtue they attain is really no more than the ability to trade pleasure for pleasure, pain for pain. The philosopher alone is truly above such things.

True virtue always co-exists with wisdom, whether pleasure, fears, and so forth are added or taken away. When virtue is separated from wisdom and consists of the exchange of such things for each other, it is no more than an illusion, vulgar, devoid of soundness, empty of truth—and truth itself is indeed a form of purification from all these things—and *sophrosyne*, justice, courage, and wisdom are surely a form of purification. (69 b–c)

The philosopher's life as Plato presents it here is a determined quest for truth; he must detach himself from bodily concerns and their propensity to distract from rational thought, to distort perception, to entrap one in hedonistic styles of life. In detaching himself from the body, the philosopher becomes able to perceive reality as it is; to die to the world of flesh and to attain an intellectual insight into reality. Truth itself helps detach him further: knowledge of reality establishes him in true virtue, since the essence of virtue is knowledge, and the philosopher who attains to the intellectual knowledge of reality possesses also the knowledge which makes virtuous conduct possible. Not only has he escaped completely from the fear of death, he, uniquely amongst men, has become capable of truly virtuous life.

To a reader of Plato's own day, the *Phaedo* must have seemed a startling and exotic work: the sharp separation of body and soul and the demand that the philosopher struggle resolutely to free himself from all the influences of the body in order to attain to a knowledge of the truth would have seemed unfamiliar and extraordinary notions challenging common sense. Indeed, there does not seem to be anything even in what we know of Pythagorean teaching that could lead directly to the extreme position Socrates adopts in this dialogue: while the *Phaedo* shows the clearest signs of strong Pythagorean influence, it represents Plato's own personal and unique response to that influence. Socrates' discussion of the nature and aim of philosophy in the *Phaedo* is more reminiscent of Hindu descriptions of the path to ultimate knowledge in the Upanishads than of anything in earlier Greek philosophical or religious thought.

In the latter part of the *Phaedo* Socrates offers a series of arguments for the eternal existence of the soul. The view of the nature of philosophy Socrates has presented in the dialogue would have little force unsupported by convincing arguments for the soul's immortality. The whole aim of the philosopher's life as he presents it is to free himself from the disturbing and distorting influence of the obsessive pattern of physical pleasures and pains. The fulfilment of the philosopher's life would be a state of pure intellectual activity, a clear insight into the nature of reality. Since the body is the principal obstacle to the philosopher's endeavour, then existence as a pure disembodied intellect would seem to be the ultimately desirable state; such a state is possible only if the intellect can survive the death of the body.

Let us consider, then, whether the souls of the dead exist in Hades or whether they do not. We remember the ancient story—they go hence to that place, then they come back again, reborn from the dead. But if this is indeed true, if the living are reborn from the dead, then surely our souls exist there, do they not? Nothing can be reborn from the non-existent—if it can be demonstrated that the living are born from the dead, then that would be sufficient proof of their existence. If matters stand otherwise, then a different account will be needed. (70 c)

Socrates now develops an argument to show that when pairs of opposites exist, the one comes to be from the other. What becomes great was once small, what becomes worse was once better. Sleeping is succeeded by waking, waking by sleeping. In the same way, from life comes death, and from death, life. If this cyclic pattern did not exist, then one of the two opposites would come to dominate. If only sleeping existed and not the cyclic process of sleeping and waking, the whole world would end up asleep.

This argument has roots in Heraclitan and in Pythagorean philosophical speculations. The opposites fascinated the early philosophers. They lacked the refined logical apparatus Aristotle developed which enabled him to distinguish contraries from contradictories; their notion of the opposites had the plasticity ideas have before they are subjected to analysis. Concepts of negation, exclusion, opposition, rejection, denial, resistance, contrast, contradiction, and contrariety had not been distinguished in a clear and systematic way. Opposites were seen as standing over and against each other, and yet as intimately linked together. For Heraclitus the whole universe expresses the creative unity of the opposites: strife and tension are fundamental structuring principles throughout the universe. The Pythagorean school developed a list of opposites in terms of which the whole universe is structured.

Socrates' argument, that the soul is immortal since life and death are opposites and opposites come into being from their opposites, is interesting but by itself seems an inadequate basis for belief in the immortality of the soul. An attempt is made to buttress it with an argument based on the doctrine of recollection which was presented in the *Meno*.

When we encounter something in sense-experience, we are led by that encounter to recollect other things, sometimes things which are like that which we have encountered, sometimes things which are not. A picture of a lyre can remind us of a lyre. The lyre itself can remind us of the lyre's owner. In those cases where we recollect something because we have encountered something similar, we always recognize whether or not the similarity is perfect. In some cases, however, we recognize that the things we encounter in this life, while similar to something of which they remind us, can never perfectly resemble it. We may recognize two pieces of wood are equal; they can never possess an equality exactly similar to the perfect equality of equality itself. We encounter things which seem equal, and call to mind equality itself, but equality itself can never be given in sense experience. Somehow we have acquired our knowledge of equality itself before our birth in a human body furnished us with the senses, by means of which we perceive the world of everyday experience.

It is not only of equality itself we acquired knowledge before we were born in the flesh: we also acquired our knowledge of beauty itself, the good itself. The soul, Socrates is arguing, exists disembodied before it ever takes on human form and has intelligence in that disembodied state. It is in its existence before birth that the soul acquires its knowledge of pure essences. This is not, of itself, an argument for the immortality of the soul, it is an argument for its pre-existence. Socrates points out that it becomes an argument for immortality when combined with his argument for a cyclic process of life and death. The argument from opposites shows the soul, the life-principle, as existing before birth and beyond death; the argument from recollection shows the soul in the existence before birth to be possessed of intelligence and capable of apprehending the realm of ultimate essences—beauty itself, good itself, equality itself.

It would not be inconsistent to argue both for the immortality of the soul and against the soul's possessing intelligence when separated from the body. The argument from recollection adds a crucially important element to the theory of the soul Plato is developing: the soul is not merely the life-principle; it is also the intellect.

Socrates now adds a further argument for the immortality of the soul: the soul is not subject to decay and decomposition since it is uncompounded. The pure essences, the good itself, beauty itself, are eternal, changeless, uniform. The soul resembles them more than it resembles the ever-changing and corruptible body.

At death the soul of the true philosopher completes the process of liberation from the trammels of the body. It lives on in a state of happiness, free from error and folly, free from fear and passion. It lives on in a state of invisible and divine existence, deathless and wise. The soul of the man who has lived a life dominated by the demands of the body becomes defiled with the pleasures and passions of the senses. At death such a soul is weighed down with its burden of defilements and is drawn back to the visible world, hovering about the graveyard. The person who has lived an evil and depraved life experiences an even worse fate; his soul is reborn in a state of existence corresponding to his vices. Gluttons and drunkards are reborn as asses, unjust tyrants as beasts and birds of prey. Those who, while not philosophers, have lived a virtuous social and civic life according to their own natural impulses and habits, attain rebirth as members of a gentle social species, bees or ants, perhaps, or even as human beings.

Clearly Plato, both here and later in the dialogue where he

presents a fuller picture of the judgement of the dead and the afterlife, is presenting us with suggestive images of the pattern of death and rebirth, rather than with a fully articulated theory. He strengthens the picture he draws by means of the fascinating argument that the death of the soul is utterly inconceivable since it is self-contradictory. Not only is the soul eternal and immortal, the statement 'the soul is immortal' is a logically necessary truth. In English translation the argument lacks the power it draws from the ambiguity of the Greek orginal for the term 'soul': the Greek *psyche* translates as 'life' or 'life-principle' in many contexts as readily as 'soul'. The expression 'dead soul' lacks the manifest paradoxicality of the expression 'dead life' or 'dead life-principle'.

Accepting that there cannot be dead soul, or even that soul cannot die, does not entail the conclusion that human beings possess immortal souls. Showing that nothing can be both X and Y does not entail that there must exist something which is both X and not-Y, nor that there must exist something which is both Y and not-X; what it does entail is that if something is X it is not also Y and that if something is Y it is not also X.

One of the arguments for the eternity of the soul in the dialogue emphasizes the uncompounded nature of the soul and infers from this its incorruptibility. The discussion of *eros* in a later dialogue, the *Symposium*, introduces an element of complexity into the soul without any apparent acknowledgement of the degree to which this undermines the argument of the *Phaedo*. The human soul in the *Symposium* is no longer a pure intellect, it is also the seat of love or desire. In the *Republic* and the *Phaedrus* Plato presents an account of the fundamental structure of the soul which adds yet a further degree of complexity, representing the soul as having three fundamental elements, intellect, desire, and *thymos* (spirit).

The *Phaedrus* contains an account of the nature of the soul which emphasizes a property of soul which, though it would be no surprise to Plato's readers, is not represented in the *Phaedo* or the *Symposium*.

Every soul is immortal since the ever-moving is immortal. Anything which moves something else or is moved by something else ceases to live when that motion ceases. Only the self-moved never ceases to move, since it cannot be separated from itself; it is, on the contrary, the fount and origin (*arche*) of motion in other things which are moved. (245 c)

Soul is the self-moving source of motion. This notion may seem strange to a modern reader of Plato but to a Greek of his own day it would have seemed quite familiar. The Greek word *psyche*, which we translate 'soul' but which in many contexts could well be translated 'life' or 'life-principle', has an abiding association in Classical Greek thought with the idea of movement: the ability to move is a characteristic property of living things.

Socrates' argument continues as follows: 'The origin does not come into existence. Everything that comes to be must come from an origin: not so the origin itself. . . . Since it does not come into existence, it must of necessity be indestructible.' If soul were destructible, then, once it has ceased to exist, there would remain no possible source of motion in the universe and the whole system would come to a terminal halt. This argument for the eternity of the soul supplements those propounded in the *Phaedo* and prepares the way for the introduction of the World-Soul as a cosmological principle in the *Timaeus*.

Socrates introduces into his discussion of the soul what is surely one of the most famous images in philosophical literature.

We ought now to say something about the soul's nature. To state exactly what the soul is would be a job for a god, and a lengthy one at that; for a human being a brief similitude will suffice. Let us talk about it in that way. Let us compare the soul to the combined forces of a team of winged horses and their charioteer. The horses and the charioteers of the gods are entirely good and of good stock, those of other beings vary. In our case, well, in the first place the charioteer drives a pair of horses, and in the second place one of these horses is noble and good and of a stock to match, while the other is of quite opposite character and breeding. Our charioteer's job is of necessity both difficult and troublesome. (246 a–b)

The charioteer and the two horses represent the three parts or elements of the human soul. Later passages in the *Phaedrus* and passages of direct psychological exposition in the *Republic* make clear the identity of the three elements in the image. The charioteer represents reason; the noble horse is *thymos*, the spirited, energetic, aspiring element in the soul; the horse of degenerate stock is appetite.

The distinction of the three elements and the curious but vivid image Plato uses to show their interaction adds greatly to the power of his psychology. The accounts of the soul in the *Phaedo* and the *Symposium* offer no real explanation of wrongdoing: a basis is now provided for such an account. The soul now appears as complex in structure and dynamic in organization. The combination of the psychological insights of the *Phaedo* and the *Symposium* left us with the soul as a love-motivated intellect: the psychology of the *Republic* and the *Phaedrus* gives us the picture of the soul as the location of the human being's struggle with him- or herself. The sense of division and conflict which is an essential aspect of human self-experience is grounded in the fundamental structure of the human soul.

In the *Phaedo* it is the body which is the source of error and wrongdoing: the philosopher strives to purify himself from the body's influences. In the *Republic* and the *Phaedrus* the propensity to evil is firmly located in an essential aspect of the structure of the soul. Self-development now centres no longer on the escape from the body and its influences; it centres rather on the establishment of order and harmony in the soul. The intellect should govern, the spirited element energize the soul's activities, the appetites be trained to seek a noble and worthy fulfilment.

The dominance of one or other of the three elements of the soul gives rise to three basically different dispositions of character: the person in whom appetite dominates becomes at best a lover of spectacle, one who delights in sensuous beauty without seeking to know its eternal archetype; the man in whom the spirited element dominates, a man of action; the person in whom intellect dominates, a philosopher. This threefold typology is rooted in Pythagorean ideas.

8

The ideal *polis*

The Athens in which Plato grew to maturity thought of itself as the supreme embodiment of the Greek ideal. During his youth, despite the degree to which the Athenians admired themselves as a free community of self-governing citizens, Athens had shown itself capable of vindictive cruelty, of contempt for human rights, of serious political and military misjudgement, of nationalistic arrogance, and of grave injustice. Socrates had taught Plato contempt for a system which chose its chief officers by lottery, a suspicion of a system which gave no place to expertise in matters of political and legal decision-making. Given the distrust of democracy he had acquired from Socrates, it is no surprise that he was drawn at first to look to his right-wing uncles to lead the city to better things. Their political incompetence, their wanton cruelty and vengefulness during the period the Thirty Tyrants were in power gave him an equal distrust of the oligarchic aristocratic tradition they represented and, to some extent, even of the Spartan government they admired. The content of the earlier dialogues, however, is of itself sufficient evidence that whatever the degree of his disillusionment with the political realities of the Athens of his own day, Plato remained deeply involved with the study of political ideas and values.

In the *Republic* Plato presents a sustained and developed discussion of the nature of the ideal form of social organization in the context of a debate on the nature of justice. Socrates constructs an account of the origin of the *polis*. Individual human beings are not self-sufficient; alone, they are unable to fulfil their own needs. Human beings gather in communities, helping each other satisfy their needs. They freely exchange mutual help to mutual advantage. A settled community of human beings co-operating together to fulfil their needs and to promote their common welfare is what we call a *polis*.

There are various different jobs which need to be done if the variety of different human needs is to be fulfilled. Human beings need food to eat, clothing to wear, houses to live in. It would be possible for an individual person to spend part of his or her time in producing food, in making clothes, in building houses. In a settled community the variety of forms of work essential to the community's economic life should ideally be performed by individuals who specialize in particular kinds of work. The specialist who applies his skills in a field of activity to which he is particularly suited can develop those skills to ensure his work is of a high standard. A settled community in which individual members specialize in work for which they are suited will provide a better basis for the fulfilment of the economic needs of its members than would a community of individuals each of whom engaged himself in the whole range of tasks required in order to provide himself with food, clothing, and shelter and to fulfil all his other needs.

A *polis* is a settled community of human beings whose economic functions are differentiated and specialized so that the needs of the members of the community are fulfilled. Such a community could be very small: Socrates argues it would be possible to have a *polis* of no more than a handful of members, since such a population would be sufficient to fulfil all the basic economic needs of the community. A farmer to produce food, a tailor and a shoemaker to produce clothing, a builder to build houses, a toolmaker to provide tools, and a merchant to trade and barter would seem to provide all the basic economic functions to allow the basic needs of a community to be met.

The social life of such a basic community would of necessity be simple. Socrates offers a delightful description: here is Jowett's translation (372 a–d):

First let us consider what will be their way of life, now that we have thus established them. Will they not produce corn, and wine, and clothes, and shoes, and build houses for themselves? And when they are housed, they will work in summer commonly stripped and barefoot, but in winter substantially clothed and shod. They will feed on barley and wheat, baking the wheat and kneading the flour, making noble puddings and loaves; these they will serve up on a mat of reeds or clean leaves, themselves reclining the while upon beds of yew or myrtle boughs. And they and their children will feast, drinking of the wine which they have made, wearing garlands on their heads, and having the praises of the gods on their lips, living in sweet society, and having a care that their families do not exceed their means; for they will have an eye to poverty or war. . . . Of course they will have a relish—salt, and olives, and cheese, and onion, and cabbages or other country herbs, which are fit for boiling; and we shall give them a dessert of figs, and pulse, and beans, and myrtle-berries, and beech nuts, which they will roast at the fire, drinking in moderation. And with such a diet they may be expected to live in peace to good old age, and bequeath a similar life to their children after them.

Glaucon, Plato's brother and one of the principal speakers in the dialogue, derides this model of the *polis* as a city for pigs rather than for people: it may fulfil the most basic and elementary of our economic needs, our survival needs, but it lacks virtually all that civilized life requires and civilized people take for granted. Socrates responds by acknowledging that his Basic *Polis* would indeed lack the luxuries we take for granted in a civilized state: the Basic *Polis* is a community working to fulfil the fundamental economic needs of human beings; it does that, and it provides a basis for the kind of social life described above. The Basic *Polis* does not provide for the fulfilment of all possible wants; it neither promotes nor satisfies human acquisitiveness. It is of necessity a frugal community.

Recent commentators tend to interpret the Basic *Polis* as an ideal type, a model constructed in such a way as to disclose the fundamental economic structure of every *polis*. An important argument in favour of this is that there is no account offered in the *Republic* of the political (as opposed to the economic) structure of the Basic *Polis*. This does seem to suggest that Plato has no particular interest in the politics of the Basic *Polis*, and is using it as no more than a model which discloses the most fundamental economic structure required in a settled human community.

Unfortunately, such an interpretation of the Basic *Polis* faces an important textual obstacle. Socrates explicitly says (372 e): 'The true *polis* seems to me to be the one we have described, like a person in good health—but if you want us to study the city in a feverish state, there's nothing to stop us.' This comment cannot be dismissed. For one thing it coheres with and reflects what we know of the simple frugality of Socrates' own life, the moral ideals of a purified and virtuous life for which Plato has him argue in the *Phaedo*, and the psychological indications in the *Republic* itself that the appetitive aspect of the personality needs to be restrained if the human being is to act in a rational and morally upright way.

If Plato has Socrates diagnose the difference between the Basic *Polis* and the Luxurious State described in the body of the *Republic* as based on acquisitiveness and greed, then, unless it can be shown that Socrates should here be interpreted as speaking ironically, we are left with a clear indication that Plato sees the Luxurious State, the Civilized *Polis*, as distinguished from the Basic *Polis* in that its economic structure is developed beyond that of the Basic *Polis* precisely in order to pander to the worst in human character, the lowest element in the human personality.

When Socrates begins to develop his model to meet Glaucon's objection to the quality of life in the Basic *Polis*, among the first new economic functions he introduces are those of the doctor and the soldier.

'And shall we not find doctors a necessity—all the more so, given the way we are now living, than we did before?'

'Indeed.'

'And the amount of land that was sufficient to support the population before will now be too small?'

'Undeniably.'

'So we shall need to chop off a slice of our neighbours' territory if we want enough for pasture and cultivation—and they will want a slice of ours, if they too go beyond the limits of necessity and set out on the path of unbounded acquisitiveness?'

'That will certainly happen, Socrates.'

'Then we shall be at war, Glaucon, won't we?'

'Indeed.'

'Well then, without going into the good or evil effects of war, we have at least uncovered its origin to be identical with that of most of the evils that exist in cities, whether individual or public.'

'Undoubtedly.'

'Then our *Polis* will need a considerable addition—an entire army to go and fight against invaders for all the things we have just been talking about.'

It is significant that Socrates interprets the richer life of the Luxurious State as requiring two new specialisms; one to cope with ill health the richer lifestyle will produce, one to cope with the need for territorial aggrandizement which will now ensue. The implication of this is clear; the Basic *Polis*, being a frugal community, is a healthy community, the Civilized State has health problems because of its richer lifestyle; the frugal community has nothing to raise envy in others, nothing to provoke acquisitive greed. The frugal community has no need of doctors and soldiers: they would be redundant.

Doctors and soldiers are needed to solve problems caused by the lifestyle of the Civilized State. The same is true of the system of government of the Civilized State. Whatever the degree of attention Plato gives to the government of the Civilized State, whatever the emphasis he lays on the education of its rulers, whatever the degree to which it is the very model of social justice, we are forced to acknowledge that the Civilized State's need for a system of government is founded on its moral inferiority to the Basic *Polis*.

It is the Basic *Polis*, the Frugal Community, which can most fully embody Plato's moral ideal. Imagine a community of what he would regard as true philosophers, a community of men and women who have escaped from the fuddled illusions of the unpurified and uneducated life and attained insight into the intelligible realm. How would such a community live? They would have no interest in the acquisition of material wealth, no interest in a life of sensuous pleasure. A community of true philosophers would live a frugal life, providing for the body's basic needs as a matter of duty, but avoiding the luxuries that can awaken the appetitive element of the soul and lead to moral deterioration. A community of persons in love with truth can have no interest in the fine things which Glaucon sees as essential to civilized life.

Plato's philosopher, who has attained insight into the eternal intelligible world of which the material, sensuous world is but a transient image, does not look to material things to fulfil his highest needs. His basic survival needs will be met, as they must be, by recourse to material things, food, clothing, shelter. Once these basic survival needs are fulfilled, he would have no reason to seek for more material possessions to provide him with pleasure and comfort. Why should he wish to make himself more at home in the world of material things where he knows he is a temporary exile? The philosopher's need is to maintain and continually renew his awareness of the intelligible world, the world of Forms. The philosopher finds his fulfilment in the knowledge of Truth, Beauty, and Goodness, not in possession of material luxuries.

The Basic *Polis* provides for all the philosopher's material needs: the Civilized State offers him the fulfilment of the same needs, but in addition surrounds him with unnecessary material things which, as sources of comfort and pleasure, provide him with no more than an array of dangerous temptations.

The Frugal Community is defined solely in economic and not in political terms for an important but not immediately obvious reason. The Frugal Community may need no system of government: a community based on the free exchange of goods, skills, and services to meet basic human needs lacks precisely those luxuries which lead to immorality and to the need for rulers and systems of law. The Frugal Community can be a society where reason rules, where conflicts are settled by reasoned arbitration; where laws need not be formulated, the moral quality of life in the community making them unnecessary.

I am not arguing that any community which had the economic structure of the Basic *Polis* would of necessity have no system of government, only that it is not necessary that a Basic *Polis* would have a system of government. The Basic *Polis* can exist as an economic community and a social community without being in the modern sense of the word a state.

The Civilized *Polis* must be a state if it is to survive. Its material opulence is sufficient to ensure the existence of whole categories of inhabitants strongly motivated by acquisitiveness and greed. Systems of law will be necessary to restrain the acquisitive impulse of the inhabitants, systems of defence to fend off the acquisitiveness of outsiders. Wealth necessitates systems of coercion.

It is not safe to assume that Plato is being frivolous when he makes Socrates assert that the Basic *Polis* is 'the true *polis*'. The brevity of treatment it receives should not blind us to the significance of this simple society. To Glaucon the inhabitants of the Basic *Polis* live like pigs: to a true philosopher they live precisely the kind of life he would choose for himself. A Frugal Community of true philosophers would be the Ideal Society: an anarchic community where the soul is liberated by the simplicity of the society's material life, where there is no fear of invasion since there is nothing to tempt an invader, no need for systems of coercive law since there is no wealth to create the basis for the conflicts of material interests that require coercive solutions to disagreements. The Basic *Polis* can at its best be a sharing community of rational persons devoted to each other's good. Such a society would be morally preferable to any Civilized State, even the Ideal State depicted in the *Republic*. The Ideal State is precisely that: not the Ideal Society of the Ideal Community, merely the Ideal State. If an Ideal Community should ever exist it would have the economic structure of the Basic *Polis* and would have no need to be a state.

Plato's discussion of the Basic *Polis* is intended to identify the economic basis of all societies: the association of human beings to fulfil the needs each is individually unable to fulfil and the division of labour which enables the members of the society to devote their energies to the work for which each is suited. In the Basic *Polis* the range of tasks which need to be performed is derived from the survival needs of human beings. The richer and more complex range of goods and services demanded in a Civilized State requires a much wider range of specialisms, greater material resources, and above all more territory.

The Frugal Community is a small, simple society united by the members' need of each other, and by the simplicity of the life they share. Envy and jealousy would find it hard to take root. Once a rich lifestyle is established and individuals or groups can acquire wealth, serious conflicts of interest can occur. A Civilized State needs to maintain its unity: it needs a form of organization and government to unite the citizens in a stable social structure.

Plato's solution to the problem of the ideal structure of the Civilized State is the division of the citizens into three classes, each of which has its own specialized function: the Rulers will govern the state, warrior Auxiliaries will support and assist the Rulers, the Third Class, the rest of the citizens, will provide the whole range of goods and services required for civilized life. The Rulers and Auxiliaries are the Guardians of the state. The Ideal State differs from the Basic *Polis* in two main ways; the Third Class will include citizens who practise the entire range of special-isms required in the Basic *Polis* and in addition will include citizens specializing in a wide range of tasks not required in the Basic *Polis*; the Basic *Polis* has no political or governmental structure, the Ideal State has an army and a ruling class to defend and govern the state.

Since the Ideal State needs to maintain its unity, its Guardian classes must be taught to love the *polis*, and devote themselves to its service. Both Rulers and Auxiliaries need to be motivated by the conviction they should act in all circumstances in the best interests of the *polis* as a whole. The Rulers must hold even more firmly to this conviction than their Auxiliaries.

Plato surrounds his Guardians with strict rules. They are to have no personal wealth and no family ties. They will undergo an education designed to develop the qualities of character to fit them for their task. The Guardians need to develop a loving concern for the well-being of their fellow citizens together with a capacity for spirited action when the need arises. They need to attain a balance amongst the three elements of their souls, a harmony of intellect and spirit so they can act with courage and self-restraint, and a harmony of appetite and intellect so that they find the fulfilment of their aspirations in the devoted service of the community and in friendship with their peers.

Male and female Guardians will have the same education and carry out the same duties. In Book V of the *Republic* Socrates faces the objection that men and women differ in nature and are therefore suited to different kinds of work. His answer is that the difference between men and women are bodily differences; a person's suitability for a particular kind of work depends on the person's qualities of mind and character. Plato believed that the Athens of his day wasted the talents of half its population: an Ideal State would give women an equal opportunity with men in military and governmental work.

The Guardians have neither private property nor family ties.

The family is not only a kinship structure, it is also a focus of loyalty. Kinship ties played an important social and political role in Plato's Athens: he evidently saw the family as a divisive social institution and one incompatible with the existence of rulers totally committed to the well-being of the state as a whole. The Rulers are to carry out a careful breeding programme; they will stage-manage mating lotteries which will give participants the impression they are mated at random; in reality couples will be mated on eugenic grounds, incestuous matings will be avoided, and combinations effected which produce the finest possible crop of children.

The Guardian classes will be united by the abolition of the family. Adult Guardians will regard every child as their own; children will regard every adult Guardian as a parent. All Guardians will regard each other as kin. The narrow loyalty of the family is replaced by a kin-bonding of the entire Guardian class.

Since the members of the Guardian classes will have no private property, but will share all things, there will be no basis for dissension amongst them. People of the Third Class will have their own property and their own families. Measures will be taken to ensure individuals and groups do not lapse into utter poverty or acquire a dangerous excess of personal wealth. The members of the Third Class will have the resources at their disposal to live the sort of life they desire. The Third Class encompasses every kind of work other than the tasks of government and soldiery. Members of the Third Class may as individuals be highly intelligent or courageous, but it is not essential they should be so: the life-style of the Third Class will provide an appropriate satisfaction for the man or woman in whom the appetitive element of the soul is particularly strong.

The three classes function in the Ideal State in a way analogous to that in which the three elements of the personality function in an individual. The Ruling Class will be the intellect of the state, the warrior-Auxiliaries the expression of courage and spirit, the Third Class the power of appetite. In individual life, the three elements must be brought into order if the person is to attain moral health. The political health of the state requires that the three classes exist in a harmonious and ordered relationship under the governing and ordering control of the ruling class.

In order to maintain the stability of the state, Socrates suggests that the Rulers make use of a 'fine fiction', a simple myth taught to all citizens. All human beings are kin, born of the one earth, but differing in the metal which dominates their constitution. In some gold predominates, in some silver, in some bronze or iron. Each type of constitution has its own proper function in the life of the community. The worst that could happen to the state would be to be ruled by a person in whom bronze or iron predominates.

None the less, Plato is prepared to accept a certain degree of social mobility. Children will be tested early in life: should a child of the Guardian classes turn out to be unsuitable for the life and work of that class, it will be brought up as a member of the Third Class. Should parents of the Third Class produce children of exceptional natural endowments, then their children will be accepted into the Guardian class and educated as Guardians.

Another form of social mobility will also exist: if members of the Guardian class show themselves to be cowardly in battle, then they will be reallocated to the Third Class and required to carry out appropriate work, as, for example, farmers or craftsmen.

Plato was not under the illusion that his Ideal State could last for ever. He admits that it will inevitably deteriorate and its perfect constitution be replaced by an imperfect pattern of social organization and government. The constitution of the Ideal State is none the less designed to promote permanence and stability; potential sources of conflict are minimized. No state existing in Plato's day even approximated to the Ideal State: he recognized that it might never be established in all its perfection. The *Republic* describes an ideal form of social organization: the description both embodies the design of an ideal system and functions as an Ideal Model to which existing states can be compared and their deficiencies thereby identified.

Plato presents the *Republic* as a dialogue on the nature of justice: the Ideal State is presented as the social embodiment of justice. The division of functions in the state is the principle which expresses the nature of justice. A just social order is one in which order and harmony are maintained in society by each class of citizens carrying out the tasks to which they are suited and not interfering with the work of others.

9

Educating the ruling class

The citizens of the Ideal State will differ in their natural capacities and dispositions; they will specialize in work for which they are naturally suited. Members of the Guardian classes need specific attributes of character if they are to operate effectively and to maintain a stable society. Both Rulers and Auxiliaries need to be courageous and resolute and to develop a profound loving commitment to the welfare of all their fellow citizens: Rulers and Auxiliaries alike must be virtuous men and women. For Plato, men and women become virtuous if and only if they have correct views as to what is right and wrong, good and evil, just and unjust, wise and foolish. Virtuous conduct exists only when grounded in true knowledge or right opinion. The acquisition of sound views requires an effective system of education to inculcate and ground those views.

The method of education outlined in the *Republic* is based upon Plato's understanding of human psychology, his analysis of the structure of human personality. The content of the system of education is derived from his theoretical understanding of the ultimate nature of reality and of the cognitive ladder by which it is possible to ascend from the world of illusory images to the intuition of the Good itself. The aim of the education prescribed for the Guardians is twofold: the physical, moral, and intellectual development of the individual and the production of classes of Rulers and Auxiliaries who have the personal qualities, the physical and mental abilities, the attitudes and dispositions, the skills and the knowledge required for the execution of the Guardians' duties. The education of those who are to govern and guard the state is too important to be left, as in Plato's Athens, to private initiative and personal decision; a state system is to be established. A state system existed in Sparta and some details of that system find echoes in the system Socrates is made to propose: the system of education in the Ideal State is, however, utterly different in spirit from the Spartan system.

The children of the Guardian class follow a curriculum with three elements, *mousike, gymnastike*, and mathematics. The successful development of the child's character depends on a balance being maintained amongst these three curricular elements.

(a) Mousike—liberal arts

Plato believed that the literary, visual, and musical arts have an immense power to shape and form character. They have, therefore, an important role to play in education. Stories, songs, poems, plays, instrumental music, works of visual art are not merely objects of aesthetic interest; they are meaningful, they express ideas and values and emotions. To expose a child to a random collection of literary, musical, and visual art-works is educational folly; it is exposing the child's mind and personality to the formative influence of a random collection of ideas, values, and emotions which are all the more powerful given the attractive and delightful qualities art-works possess. Any sound educational system involves the most careful selection of the art-works to which children are to be exposed.

Stories are important to children. In Plato's day, Athenian children were brought up on a heady diet of myths and legends, especially on the stories embedded in the poems of Homer and Hesiod. The education system proposed for the Guardians involves the rejection of virtually the entire corpus of Homer and Hesiod: lies about the gods are unsuitable as educational materials.

Plato insists that stories about gods and heroes must be truthful: the god is perfect, immutable, utterly truthful. Stories of divine immorality, of gods who are shape-changing deceivers, thieves, liars, and adulterers have no place in education. In arguing thus, Plato is following in the footsteps of Xenophanes and Heraclitus, both of whom were harshly critical of the foolish stories told about the gods. Interpreters of the myths had attempted to meet such criticisms by producing elaborate allegorical interpretations of the myths which gave them an acceptable meaning. Plato refuses to accept that the existence of such interpretations justifies the use of the myths and legends he condemns. The story itself has the power to influence the child apart from the interpretations placed on it.

The stories used in the education of young children must have a suitable moral content. They must not undermine the moral development of the child by portraying gods and heroes as indulging in immoral conduct; they must not show evildoing as a source of happiness or virtuous conduct leading to misery. They must promote virtuous conduct. Stories which encourage dishonesty, cowardice, intemperance, or injustice must be eliminated, together with stories which encourage excessive frivolity.

In the case of dramatic representations the greatest caution is required; it is bad enough that acting a role requires one to be, as it were, two persons at once; if the role involves the acting-out of morally unworthy actions it endangers the moral health of the actor. Acting out the role of a morally upright character and representing dramatically his good deeds is permissible, otherwise acting has no educational value and narrative should replace dramatic representation in all other cases.

Poetry, song, and music too have their importance in developing character. Dirges and lamentations, however, have no educational value, nor has any form of music which leads to self-indulgence, softness, idleness, or the drunken abandonment of self-control. We are educating warriors and rulers, not sensualists and voluptuaries. The more restrained and sober tones of the lyre are to be preferred to the wilder emotions of the flute. The martial vigour of the Dorian mode and the sober beauty of the Phrygian will provide us with the full range of melodies we shall need: the mournful qualities of the Mixolydian and Hyperlydian and the febrile sensuousness of the Ionian and Lydian modes make all four of them educationally undesirable.

The developing child should be surrounded by artefacts which embody and express order, harmony, and beauty. In this way the senses themselves become a means of moral and intellectual education. The young Guardian-to-be acquires a taste for order, harmony, and proportion. A developed appreciation of beauty is itself morally educative. Goodness and beauty are ultimately one.

An education based on truth, order, and harmony not only encourages the development of virtuous conduct, aesthetic appreciation, and rational thought, it provides the young Guardian-to-be with an ability to discern those qualities of physical, moral, and intellectual beauty which make another worth seeking as a friend. Friendship is both part of education and one of its objects: 'upright love is to love the orderly and the beautiful in a self-controlled and cultured manner' (403 a). Beauty of character should attract us, even when combined with physical defects. Love based on the discernment of another's fine qualities may well express itself in physical affection, but it must not be allowed to degenerate into sexual licence. Sexual indulgence would lead to sensuous excesses, to a frenzied hedonism entirely inappropriate to the formation of the character of young warriors and rulers. The basis of true friendship is that love of beauty which is the content and end of liberal education.

(b) *Gymnastike*—physical training

The balanced character required of a member of the Guardian classes cannot be attained by literary, musical, and artistic education alone; a balancing measure of challenging physical education is also required. The young Guardians should be trained to a high standard of athletic ability and specifically should undergo a training which prepares them for war.

The physical training provided for the young Guardians should be simple and straightforward, aimed at producing a sound state of physical health. Elaborate diets, fine foods, or elegant confections are not required. The young people must be prepared for the privations they may have to face in the field, not trained in self-indulgence and valetudinarianism.

Socrates is made to argue that the function of doctor and jurist should be to promote and maintain health where it already exists, not to attempt to produce it where it is absent.

The medical provision and the system of justice which you will lay down as law for the states will provide treatment for those who are of sound body and soul; as for the rest, those whose bodies are unsound will be left to die, those whose souls are unsound and beyond cure will be put to death. (409 e–410)

Medicine and law should promote good health and prevent ill health. At least in so far as concerns the Guardian classes, that should be possible, since the educational regime they undergo is designed to avoid the sicknesses to which a luxurious lifestyle so easily leads. Their education is cathartic: it purges them of the influence the sight of material riches could have on their characters.

Besides the regime of simple diet and strenuous physical training which is proposed as a means of preparing the young Guardians for the performance of their duties, Socrates adds a further detail: even as children they are to be taken to watch military engagements when they occur, to learn by observation the reality of their place in society.

(c) Mathematics

The study of the mathematical disciplines provides the basis of the higher education of the Guardians. Mathematics provides a sound training in rational thought; it explores the pattern of intelligible numerical and quantitative relations. It is the gateway to the world of the Forms and to true knowledge.

The mathematical sciences which the Guardians will study are arithmetic, plane geometry, solid geometry, astronomy, and harmonics. The inclusion of the last two should not mislead us: Plato is concerned with the abstract mathematical aspects of astronomy and harmonics, not with observational science.

The initial stages of mathematical education will begin in childhood, not by compulsion, but by means of educational play. When the young Guardians are plunged into a demanding programme of physical training at the age of seventeen or eighteen, mathematical studies will be left aside. At the age of twenty the young Guardians will be tested to see whether they possess the aptitude for the most advanced stages of education.

The mathematical part of the curriculum provides the student with knowledge of eternal realities, unchanging patterns of relations. The mathematical studies the young Guardians pursue lead them by the use of visible diagrams to pure abstract reasoning about number, figure, movement, proportion. Mathematics links the world of the senses with the world of Forms: we begin by studying diagrams, we end by inferring the nature of mathematical relations which give us knowledge of mathematical Forms. Such knowledge is valuable of itself and mathematical study is a powerful educational device. Socrates emphasizes too that mathematics is an important study for military personnel.

The pattern of education Socrates is made to prescribe for the young Guardians is specifically designed to ensure they do not suffer from the moral laxity and physical idleness endemic in a luxurious state. Severe control of the stories, poetry, music, and artefacts which influence the young Guardians is all the more essential in that the lifestyle of the Third Class will present serious temptations for any Guardian whose moral development has been marred by exposure to the corrupting influences of mournful songs, foolish legends, myths of divine immorality, or voluptuous flute music. Throughout their childhood and youth the Guardians need a programme of education of the kind Socrates lays down in order to guard them against the dangers inherent in the degree of luxury allowed into the Ideal State.

The system of education is a state system: it is organized and maintained by the rulers to serve the political needs of the state; it is part of the Guardian classes' system of reproduction. Interference with the system of education could have the most disastrous consequences for the constitutional stability of the state.

The description of the general education of the Guardian classes develops the therapeutic metaphor presented in the *Gorgias*. Plato is caught between the vision of the Ideal State as a therapeutic community containing in its legal and educational systems the means of inculcating physical and moral health, and the realization that all existing states were riddled with a depressing variety of moral and political diseases. The state as it exists is a sorry affair, but the state ought to be and could be a training ground in virtue, its laws a system of moral education, its constitution the expression of justice in terms of social order.

In Books VIII and IX of the *Republic* Plato presents the pattern of deterioration which leads to the degenerate forms of political constitution, Timarchy, Oligarchy, Democracy, and Tyranny. It is significant that the account he offers of the origins of Timarchy, the first and mildest degree of political degeneration, is based on a defect in the education of the ruling class. If the education of the Rulers overemphasizes physical training and instils in them an excessively warlike outlook, then the ruling class will become divided against itself and political power will fall into the hands of aggressive, honour-loving groups. As they age, the rulers of the Timocratic state will develop an increasing taste for wealth and luxury. As wealth becomes the object of political interest, the Timocracy is replaced by an Oligarchy of plutocrats. In an Oligarchy the last vestiges of the Ideal State are gone: the Oligarchy is not one state but two, a City of the Rich dominating a City of the Poor. When excessive greed has destabilized the Oligarchic state, warfare arises amongst the classes of the state; when the poor overthrow the rich, a Democracy is created. In a Democracy, every citizen is his own ruler; the Democratic State has no consistent policy, no effective system of law. When a man arises who can persuade the mass of the people to choose him as leader against the wealthier classes who continually seek to re-establish an Oligarchy and the class of drones that spend all their time playing politics, a Tyranny will be established, and the worst of all forms of government will now afflict the state.

Plato's account of the degeneration of the state is grounded in the psychological damage inflicted by defects in the education system. The education system is an essential part of the constitutional structure of the Ideal State. It is essential for psychological reasons: once luxuries have been allowed into the state the most careful programme of education is essential to ensure the Guardian classes acquire psychological stability, firmness, and balance of character, the right relation amongst the elements of personality.

The philosopher ruler is a man or woman whose personality is ordered under the rule of intellect (*nous*): the Tyrant is dominated not only by appetite (*epithymia*) but by the lowest and most ungovernable aspect of appetite, *eros*.

The first stages of education may well be enough of themselves to provide the state with warriors it can trust, but they would not be adequate for the education of the Rulers. The first stage would provide a basic liberal education, a sound physical training, and a basic mathematical education, and would develop the young

Guardians' characters so that they could carry out their duties. The Rulers need to advance beyond the right opinion which is enough to enable the practice of the virtues, to genuine knowledge of the nature of values: in the case of the Supreme Rulers, to the knowledge of the Good Itself if a just social order is to be maintained and sound laws enacted. The basic mathematical education needs to be extended and developed to enable the Rulers to understand something of the ultimate pattern of reality.

The 20-year-olds who are found suitable for promotion face further studies. They are to study the interconnection of the subjects they studied as children. They have acquired a wide range of information from their literary, cultural, and mathematical studies; the collection of pieces of information they have needs now to be synthesized and brought into order, so that they can attain a synoptic view of the body of information they possess. Their studies will extend beyond the horizontal interrelationships of the various bodies of information they have acquired, to explore the relation of what they have learned to reality. The success or failure of the students in these studies will furnish evidence of their suitability for the study of dialectic.

Plato offers no account of exactly what is involved in this initial stage of advanced study: it will be sufficient to occupy the young Rulers-to-be for a solid ten years. Perhaps we are to see the students learning from tutors who have advanced far in the study of dialectic, who can explain to them as much of the structure of the intelligible world as can be grasped by students who have not yet acquired the skills of dialectical reasoning which will lift them to knowledge of the Idea of the Good. Perhaps, too, they will develop their studies of the mathematical sciences to a higher and higher degree. Presumably the most advanced levels of the mathematical sciences lead to the contemplation of theorems of great generality which enable the students to draw together wide ranges of mathematical knowledge. No doubt at this initial stage of advanced education students will be 'inducted into' the practice of forms of reasoning quite unknown at lower levels of study.

We are to presume that the promoted students engage themselves in practical affairs as well as study. At the age of 30 a further process of selection takes place: those who have been most assiduous in the performance of their duties, who have applied themselves most strenuously to their course of study, who have made the best showing in battle, will be chosen to study dialectic.

Exactly what Plato means by 'dialectic' in the *Republic* is rather difficult to determine. In the earlier dialogues it is clear that dialectic is formally identical with eristic. The use of continual systematic questioning to reduce the proponent of a thesis to self-contradiction is eristic; the tedious verbal acrobats Euthydemus and Dionysodorus provide a distressing exhibition of eristic at its silliest and emptiest in the *Euthydemus*. The use of continual systematic questioning to subject a statement to consistency-testing is dialectic; the Socrates of the early dialogues shows how effective a test dialectical questioning can provide, and what a range of insights dialectical questioning can generate. Formally the patterns of questioning used by Euthydemus and Dionysodorus and by Socrates are indistinguishable.

The *Meno* has, in Plato's view, shown that systematic questioning can lead beyond bewildered ignorance to sound opinion, and eventually to knowledge. Whatever the nature of the dialectic studied by the Rulers, it cannot be identified totally with the dialectic of the earlier dialogues nor with the questioning discussed in the *Meno*. Dialectic in the *Republic* leads to knowledge of the Forms, ultimately to knowledge of the Form of the Good, and thence to conclusions which can be drawn in the light of the knowledge of the Good the Rulers have acquired. The dialectic of the early dialogues and the persistent systematic questioning of the *Meno* have no such function.

It is unlikely, however, that the dialectic the Rulers study is totally unrelated to the dialectic of the early dialogues. A comment Socrates makes on the undesirable effects which the study of dialectic can have upon young men is devoid of point if the dialectic to which he refers is something totally unfamiliar to Plato's readers.

The method of dialectic, Socrates informs us, is to remove hypotheses or postulates. It makes use of pure reason, unaided by the senses and is the path to the attainment of knowledge of the

Good Itself. Since the Good Itself is the principle of intelligibility in virtue of which the Forms are knowable, the successful dialectician who attains knowledge of the Good is uniquely capable of attaining a synoptic view of the whole intelligible realm.

Dialectic begins where mathematics ends: it begins with theoretical theses which are derived as the conclusions of a process of hypothetical deduction; it then subjects these to systematic questioning, seeking for the principles which underlie them and in which they are grounded. It will repeat this systematic intellectual questioning, treating the principles so uncovered as hypotheses and seeking the more basic principles in which they in turn are grounded. It proceeds in this way until the dialectician uncovers the first principle which is the ground of all truth, the Idea of the Good. Once the dialectician attains insight into the nature of the Good Itself he or she can infer the exact nature of the other Forms and the structure of the relationships amongst the Forms.

Dialectic terminates in understanding. Insight into the nature of the Good is the supreme cognitive experience available to human beings, and it does not reduce the dialectician to illuminated silence; quite the contrary, it gives him or her a theoretical understanding which can be put into words and tested:

If a person is unable to define the Idea of the Good in such a way that by the account he gives of it he distinguishes it from all others, and then make his way through all 'refutations' as if he were in a battle—resolutely refuting them not on the basis of opinion but on the basis of reality, holding firmly to his account as he proceeds—surely you wouldn't say such a person knows the Good as it really is (or any other good for that matter!) (534 b–d)

The dialectician who has attained the knowledge of the Good should be able to state what the Good is, and to defend his account against all attempted refutations. This surely gives us a picture of the intellectual vitality of the ruling class Plato envisages: the attainment of the aspiring dialecticians will be tested out by the systematic questioning familiar to us from the early dialogues. Not only are the philosopher-rulers required to know the Good, they must be able to demonstrate their knowledge to their peers.

Once the dialectician has attained an understanding of the nature of the Good, he or she can study the nature of the whole array of Ideas which depend on the Good for their existence and intelligibility. This form of study would be an a priori science of the ultimate nature of reality, a pure deductive metaphysics.

Parmenides' poem *The Way of Truth* may well have provided Plato with a model of the descending dialectic. From a single principle *esti* ('it is'), Parmenides deduces his account of Being: he reasons dialectically to the conclusion that reality is a single, eternal, unchanging sphere of being. Plato regarded Parmenides with a particular reverence and knew his poem well; he quotes it on several occasions. Plato did not accept all Parmenides' conclusions, but he did believe that Parmenides had made a major contribution to philosophy. His method of dialectical reasoning seems sufficiently similar to the process of reasoning Plato describes for it to be regarded as at least its prototype.

The dialectician, then, is able to explore the ultimate structure of reality, and to understand the basic principles of all fields of knowledge. He has acquired knowledge from which the solution to society's problems can, in principle, be derived.

10

The theory of Forms or Ideas

Heraclitus described the majority of men as wandering about in a sleeplike state, following their own opinions: they need to awake from their dreams, put aside the prejudices which distort their perceptions of reality and apply themselves to acquiring knowledge of the objective order of reality. The Eleatic school presented pure dialectical reason as the means by which such knowledge could be obtained: the unreliable data the senses provide are put aside in favour of the conclusions attained by a process of abstract intellectual thought. The Pythagoreans aimed at the contemplative intuition of the mathematical patterns which underlie the whole order of the experienced universe by means of a rigorous programme of physical, mental, and spiritual *katharsis*. In the great dialogues of Plato's middle period we see the synthesis and transcendence of the influence each of these philosophical schools has exercised on his thought.

The early dialogues had shown cultured and educated men to be utterly incapable of defending their definitions of moral, political, or aesthetic concepts in the face of the consistency-test of Socrates' dialectical questioning. His questioning discloses how ill-founded are the opinions that people are prepared to accept as the basis of personal and civic life. Professional educators, sophists, *rhetors*, and rhapsodes fare no better than bewildered boys and enthusiastic old soldiers.

The *Meno* has offered hope: the theory of recollection proposes the possibility of escaping from the dreamworld of unfounded opinions by means of the recovery of the knowledge of reality which our souls once possessed before we came to birth in the material world and became trapped in its web of sensuous pleasure and pain. In the *Meno* recollection is attained by means of questioning: mental fuddle is reduced to pure ignorance by questioning; the bewilderment brought about by collapsing certainty energizes ignorance so that further questioning can lead to the attainment of true opinion, which can become genuine knowledge if the opinion is given firm foundations by rigorous investigation into its grounding.

Socrates' arguments in the *Phaedo* show the ways in which recollection can be stirred by the objects given in sense-experience. The dialogue suggests, in effect, that sense-objects could have at least some significance in the quest for knowledge: they can at least prompt us to recollect the realities we knew before birth. This theme is poorly developed in Plato's writings: even though Plato later modifies the sharply intellectualist hostility to the body evidenced in the cathartic theory of philosophy for which Socrates argues in the *Phaedo*, he never exploits to the full the possibility that a more positive view of the cognitive role of the senses might be developed on the basis of the theory of recollection. The possibility recurs, however, both in the *Symposium* and in the *Phaedrus*, since both dialogues emphasize the power of beauty, even the sensuous beauty of physical objects. In both dialogues the beauty of physical things has a capacity to lead us beyond itself to the intuition of that Beauty of which it is a shifting, transient, partial image. It recurs too in the *Republic* in the recognition given to the importance of the aesthetic qualities of the artefacts, the music, and the stories which surround a child in its formative years. It remains none the less true that Plato does not follow to the end the implications of these insights into the value of sensory experience.

The most important advance on the theory of learning as it is proposed in the *Meno* is provided by the theory of Ideas or Forms. The theory of recollection is a theory of how we come to know; it is not, of itself, a theory of the status of the objects of knowledge. The theory of Ideas fills out and extends the theory of recollection, by providing an account of the nature of the objects of knowledge.

The *Phaedo* contains the earliest exposition of the theory of Ideas. The manner of the exposition is carefully designed to suit the flowing conversational style of the dialogue: at several points in the conversation Socrates takes the opportunity to develop one aspect after another of the theory, integrating each in turn into his discussion of immortality. The theory is not expounded in a systematic way; even the language in which it is presented varies from one part of the dialogue to another.

Socrates' account of the Ideas can be summarized as follows:

(*a*) Truth cannot be attained by the senses: reality can be apprehended by process of intellectual reasoning.

(*b*) The Just, The Beautiful, and The Good (etc.) all exist as realities inaccessible to the senses.

(*c*) The world of sense-experience contains likenesses of realities (e.g. of Equality Itself) which have no perfect manifestation in the material world.

(*d*) When we recognize that something in the world of sense-experience resembles Equality Itself (or any other reality of the kind specified in (*c*)) our knowledge of Equality Itself has not come from sense-experience: we are recollecting it from knowledge of Equality Itself which we acquired before birth.

(*e*) Realities such as The Beautiful Itself or Equality Itself are eternal and unchanging.

(*f*) These eternal realities are the Forms or Ideas which instances in the world of the senses resemble, and in which they participate.

(*g*) The Ideas or Forms are intelligible.

(*h*) True knowledge is knowledge of the eternal Ideas.

(*i*) Only the Ideas can provide adequate causal explanations.

(*j*) Individual entities can participate in a variety of Ideas: those Ideas in which an individual entity necessarily participates define its essential properties, those in which it happens to participate at a given time are its accidents.

(*k*) Individual things cannot participate in Ideas which are incompatible with the Ideas of their essential properties.

Socrates' exposition of the theory of Ideas leaves many questions unanswered. We are told there exist eternal Ideas of Beauty, Goodness, Justice, Equality, Heat, Cold, Oddness, Evenness—all of these Ideas are specifically mentioned in the *Phaedo*—but we do not know what other Ideas exist. It is, of course, possible to make a reasonable guess in many cases, but the *Phaedo* provides us with no criteria for deciding the population of the realm of eternal Ideas. Nor does the *Phaedo* provide us with any clear indication as to the exact nature of participation. Nor is it stated unambiguously exactly what kind of realities the Ideas or Forms are. They exist eternally, they are unchanging and inaccessible to sense experience, but what exactly are they? Are we to think of them as entities? If we are, then what kind of eternal entity would Equality Itself be? When we speak of the Form of Beauty or the Idea of Good it is easy to assume, without analytic reflection on the implications of the assumption, that we are dealing with eternal entities: when we speak of Equality Itself, The Just Itself, the assumption is less tempting.

Despite the considerable puzzles with which the reader is left, it is evident that the arguments of Socrates in the *Phaedo* are the vehicle of a significant theoretical development in Plato's philosophical investigations, and that his theory is being commended to the reader. It is typical of Plato that he presents a major development in a sequence of subsidiary moments in the construction of an argument about something else. The *Phaedo* is not an expository essay: the literary and dramatic form of the dialogue is exploited with immense skill and subtlety. Socrates' exposition of the theory of Ideas is smoothly integrated into a debate on the eternity of the soul to the extent that the reader may be led from stage to stage of his exposition without at first realizing he has been led by the hand through a quite unfamiliar thoughtscape. The language of the theory of Ideas is not new; its familiarity helps disguise the novelty of the theory itself.

The Ideas are intended to ground the theory of recollection on firm metaphysical and epistemological foundations. There is a world of eternal intelligible realities which the soul has known directly when in a disembodied state before its incarnation. The world we come to know by sense-experience in our present embodied life contains sensuous images of the eternal realities which can prompt us to return in recollection to the Ideas which are their eternal intelligible archetypes. The true philosopher strives continually to purify himself from the perception-distorting influence of the physical pleasures and pains to which sensuous experience gives rise, and to develop his capacity for pure intellectual thought, which alone can attain to the know-ledge of the Ideas.

Socrates' arguments in the *Symposium* are concerned with one of the Ideas, Beauty Itself. The ultimate fulfilment of the *eros* which is a fundamental element of human personality lies in the contemplation of eternal Beauty. *Eros* is 'a desire to beget of the beautiful', says Socrates: if we restrain ourselves from grasp-ing at sexual pleasure, or from merely remaining content with the delight of the companionship of a beautiful soul and even go beyond the more abstract beauty of a mathematical system, accepting none of these as the ultimate fulfilment of our *eros*, then we will be able to ascend to the creative and blissful vision of Beauty Itself. In the *Phaedrus* Socrates argues that beauty has a unique capacity to awaken in us the recollection of the world of eternal Ideas: he connects this capacity with the particular clarity and acuity of the sense of sight by which we discern the beauty of things. (This emphasis on the visual aspect of beauty may seem slightly odd, especially since Plato demonstrates elsewhere a vivid awareness of the beauty which poetry or music can possess: it reflects the tendency in the Greek thought of Plato's period to think of beauty in strongly visual terms as a kind of radiance or effulgence.)

The Idea of Beauty has a unique position in the realm of Ideas. Its image in the world of the senses prompts us more powerfully to the recollection of its eternal archetype than do the sensible images of other Ideas. The intuition of the Idea of Beauty has a unique psychological significance for human beings: the satis-faction which sexual intercourse, loving relationships, or even spiritual friendship provide is but a shadow of the spiritual fulfilment we experience in contemplating Beauty Itself. Here alone is the perfect object of love, the ultimately and absolutely desirable for its own sake.

The aesthetic ascent of the soul to the intuition of Beauty is parallel to the intellectual ascent of the soul to the knowledge of the Ideas. The two pathways are two aspects of Plato's philo-sophical spirituality.

The theory of Ideas is presented in the *Republic* by means of three celebrated images: the Sun, the Divided Line, and the Cave.

It is important to note the context in which these images are introduced: they are introduced in order to clarify exactly what kind of knowledge the philosopher-ruler of the Ideal State will require.

Socrates offers a characterization of the philosopher which shows the true philosopher to be a person ideally suited to govern. The philosopher is the person who has an intellectual grasp of eternal and changeless realities: he has acquired the certainty and stability of mind required of a ruler. The philosopher has before his mind's eye the paradigms of perfection from which criteria of value can be derived, allowing him or her to derive appropriate rules and norms for the organization of social and political life. The philosopher's love of truth is absolute, unlimited in intensity and extent. The philosopher's fulfilment is in intellectual and spiritual things, not in material wealth. Having no greed for wealth and possessions and seeing material things and embodied existence as transient, the philosopher is unafraid of death and therefore capable of the resolute and courageous action required of an effective ruler. Seeing reality as it truly is, the philosopher has a unique ability to maintain a sense of proportion in relation to all matters, an essential quality in a wise ruler.

To rule effectively, the philosopher will need to acquire a knowledge of reality adequate to the demands of his task, to come to the fullest knowledge of the Good: to attain, in so far as is possible, a perfect insight into the foundation of all value.

Socrates is asked to describe the Good, and hesitates, then offers to give an account rather of its offspring and image in the visible world, the Sun.

Socrates reminds his interlocutors of the by now familiar distinction between the many particular things which we say are beautiful or good and the Good Itself, the Beautiful Itself, the eternal Forms or Ideas in virtue of which individual beautiful things are beautiful and individual good things good. The Ideas, he reminds them, are intelligible but invisible; visible objects are unintelligible.

Sight, Socrates points out, is a complex sensory capacity. The sense of hearing requires nothing more than the presence of sound for us to be able to hear: in the case of sight, in addition to the visible object a third thing is required before we see anything, namely light. The sun is the source of light. The sun cannot, of course, be identified with the eye, nor with sight; none the less the eye is the most sunlike of the sense-organs, and its capacity to see is instilled into it by the sun. The sun is the cause of sight and is perceived by means of that capacity whose cause it is; it enables us to see, and thereby becomes visible itself.

Having expounded this account of the sun, an account which seems somewhat bizarre to a modern reader, Socrates asserts that an analogy exists between the function of the sun in relation to the visible realm and the function of the Idea of the Good in the intelligible realm. It is the Idea of the Good which gives truth to the objects of knowledge and which enables the knower to know them. It is itself knowable, but neither knowledge nor truth are identical with the Idea of the Good: it is the cause of both and transcends both.

As the sun is the source of processes of genesis, growth, and nutrition, while being itself none of these, so is the Idea of the Good the source of the existence of intelligible things.

The analogy may be awkward and unsatisfying; the main thrust of Plato's argument is, however, reasonably clear. The Idea of the Good is the supreme reality, the source of the reality of all other eternal Ideas. It is by means of the Idea of the Good that knowledge is possible: it irradiates the whole intelligible realm, enabling us to perceive the nature of the Ideas or Forms. The Idea of the Good is itself knowable as well as being the source of the knowability of all that is knowable. As it stands, this is not particularly clear or convincing; perhaps what Plato intends to convey is that knowledge has a normative dimension. Knowing an object as an instance of X-ness, as an image of the Idea of X, requires us to know what an X ought to be as well as what the various Xs happen to be. Such knowledge would depend on our ability to perceive the Idea of X in its necessary relation to the Idea of Good, that relation grounding and expressing the normative aspects of the Idea of X.

There is a parallel between the position of the Idea of the Good in the image of the Sun and the position the Beautiful Itself holds in the *Symposium* and the *Phaedrus*. The supreme fulfilment of our capacity for love is paralleled here by the supreme object of our capacity for knowledge. It might seem there is a parallelism and no more, were it not that the Socrates of the *Republic* has been at pains to point out that philosophy, the love of truth and reality, is the supreme form of love in human life as well as the supreme form of intellectual activity. This view is quite consonant with the way in which the path to the perfect fulfilment of *eros* is described in the *Symposium* and the *Phaedrus*. It is hard to resist the conclusion that the Beautiful Itself and the Idea of the Good are in some sense one.

Socrates says of the Idea of the Good that it is 'beyond being in dignity and in power' (509 b). Just as the sun, the source of generation and growth, is not itself identical with generation and growth, and indeed is not merely a principle of generation and growth, so, Plato seems to be arguing, the Idea of Good is not simply identical with being, nor is it merely the Form of Existence. What exactly Plato means by this is, to say the least, somewhat less than perfectly clear: if the Idea of the Good is the ground of the being of the other Forms, the source and cause of their reality, then it would seem to follow that the Idea of the Good is indeed the Form of Existence; the consequence of denying this would be to undermine the whole rationale of the theory of Forms; if the Form which is the source of the X-ness of other Forms is not the Form of X-ness, then we seem to be left with an impossible dilemma: either there is another Form which is the Form of X-ness but is not the cause of X-ness in other Forms, or there is no Form of X-ness at all; in neither case is it obvious how the fundamental rationale for positing the existence of the Forms could be saved, once the connection between X-ness and the Form of X-ness had been so completely severed. The safest interpretation of what Plato is saying, though it is admittedly devoid of any direct support from the text of the *Republic*, is that the Idea of the Good is beyond Being in dignity and power in that it transcends and subsumes what is meant by 'being'. On such an interpretation, the Idea of Good would also be the Form of Being, but not reducible to being merely the Form of Being.

Socrates continues his exposition of the nature of the intelligible realm and its relation to the visible by constructing a second image, the Divided Line. His interlocutors are to imagine a line divided in two unequal parts, each of which is then divided in the same proportion as that in which the original line was divided:

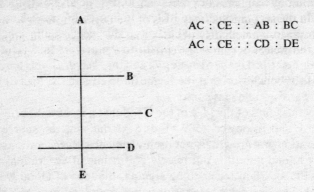

AC : CE : : AB : BC

AC : CE : : CD : DE

Socrates offers this diagram as a means of illustrating the relative degrees of clarity and obscurity in the visible and intelligible realms. The major divisions of the line separate reality from mere image, knowledge from opinion.

(a) The visible

The visible world is divided into two sections:

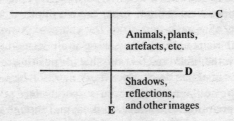

The relation of image to original (DE to CD) is analogous to that relating CE to AC. Visible things are shadows, images, and reflections of intelligible realities, relating to their originals in a way analogous to that in which the shadows, pictures, and reflections of visible things relate to the things whose shadows, images, and reflections they are. The difference in degree of clarity which marks off our cognition of the intelligible real from our cognition of the visible realm is analogous to the difference in clarity marking off our cognition of living things and artefacts from our cognition of their images. What exactly this means is not made clear in the account Socrates gives of the Divided Line: it is not, for instance, immediately obvious that we always see or apprehend the images of things less clearly than the things themselves.

(b) The intelligible

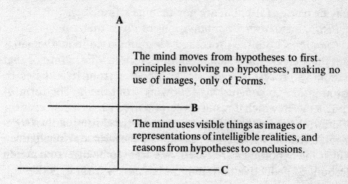

A

The mind moves from hypotheses to first principles involving no hypotheses, making no use of images, only of Forms.

B

The mind uses visible things as images or representations of intelligible realities, and reasons from hypotheses to conclusions.

C

The descriptions of sections AB and BC are, to say the least, somewhat obscure. Socrates' further exposition makes it evident that BC is the realm of mathematical reasoning, which assumes or hypothesizes the existence of odd and even numbers, of certain geometrical configurations, and so forth. When such reasoning makes use of visible things they function as images or representations of intelligible realities: the real objects of the mathematician's reasoning are the Square Itself or the Diagonal Itself, and so on. The mathematician assumes the existence of the numbers or figures about which he is thinking and arrives at conclusions about them.

Section AB represents dialectical reasoning from hypotheses treated precisely as such, as instrumental interim assumptions, and moving from them to first principles, and then down from knowledge of first principles to conclusions. All the reasoning at this level is concerned only with the Forms, never with visible things.

Socrates distinguishes four states of mind each of which corresponds to one of the four divisions of the line. The four terms Socrates uses are *noesis*, *dianoia*, *pistis*, and *eikasia*: translators have varied widely in the way they have translated them.

Eikasia, the term for the cognitive state corresponding to our apprehension of shadows and reflections, is sometimes translated 'imagination'; it means rather 'illusion', or 'conjecture', and it would not be misleading to translate it as 'fuddle'.

Pistis is belief: about the visible world we have beliefs, which may be true or false, but are not genuine knowledge.

Pistis and *eikasia* are subdivisions of *doxa*, opinion.

Dianoia is both the process of reasoning used in mathematics and the state of knowledge resulting from it. The nature of that reasoning process is clear, it is inference from hypotheses or assumptions to conclusions following from them. The form of knowledge in which it results is certain in so far as it concerns the relations between the hypotheses and the conclusions drawn from them, but never ascends to comprehend the ultimate principles on which the hypotheses are based. We seem to be offered a sketch account of deductive reasoning which moves from hypotheses it is itself unable to validate: the sort of reasoning exemplified formally in the operation of the rules of inference in an axiomatic logical or mathematical system, the axioms of which are postulates of the system, derivable within that system only by circular argument, and incapable of non-circular proof within the system.

Noesis is pure, abstract dialectical reasoning, reasoning which moves from hypothesis to first principles, from knowledge of scientific truth to the ultimate principles in which all knowledge is grounded. *Noesis* is also the state of knowledge in which we apprehend the first principles—perhaps we are tacitly invited to relate this section of the line to the distinction in levels of knowledge implied in the Sun-image, and see *noesis* in its fullest and most perfect form as knowledge of the Good Itself. That would not, of course, limit the objects of *noesis* to the Idea of the Good; it would include also the other Forms, but precisely in so far as they are known in their relation to the Idea of the Good and in relation to each other as an organized intelligible system of eternal intelligible realities dependent on and knowable in relation to the Good.

It is confusing that Plato uses the terms *dianoia* and *noesis* to name both two processes of reasoning and the two forms of knowledge in which those processes result. This should perhaps warn us that there is an element of ambiguity built into the image of the Divided Line.

We can now construct a diagram of the line showing the distinctions Socrates is making:

Cognitive states   A   Objects of cognition

KNOWLEDGE: *NOESIS*
(a) Pure, abstract, dialectical reasoning
(b) Insight into, intuition of, first principles

FORMS
—as first principles, and therefore especially the Form of the Good
—as mere hypotheses raising one to first principles

——————————————— B

KNOWLEDGE: *DIANOIA*
(a) Hypothetical deduction Mathematical reasoning Discursive Reason
(b) (Abstract) scientific knowledge

FORMS
—as mathematical hypotheses, i.e. especially those corresponding to mathematical terms and VISIBLE THINGS as images and representations

——————————————— C

OPINION: *PISTIS*
Belief

VISIBLE THINGS
Animals, plants, artefacts, etc.

——————————————— D

OPINION: *EIKASIA*
Illusion, conjecture, fuddle

VISIBLE THINGS
Shadows, images, reflections, etc.

E

The general pattern of relations exhibited in the image:
AC : CE : : AB : BC : : CD : DE.

The interpretation of the Divided Line presented here is controversial: many commentators identify the objects of *dianoia* as mathematical objects, intelligible particulars, as opposed to the Ideas which are universals. That interpretation derives from reading back into the text of the *Republic* views argued at a later

period. The text as it stands offers no support for such an interpretation, but it is impossible to prove that Plato did not have
such a view in mind.

There seems to be a general feeling amongst commentators that
the distinctions made in the lower part of the line between belief
(*pistis*) and fuddle (*eikasia*) are of little philosophical significance,
and are somewhat artificial. If one thinks of our cognition of an
individual instance of, for example, an artefact and its reflection,
then the significance of the distinction may indeed prove somewhat opaque. Once we move to consider our cognition of a group
or pattern of animals, artefacts, etc., and compare it with our
cognition of an array of shadows, reflected images, etc., a distinction of considerable philosophical interest emerges.

Consider an example. Imagine you are lying in bed on a warm
night with a brilliant street lamp shining straight into the bedroom
window. The head of the bed is towards the window; you lie facing
a plain white wall, your back to the light. Outside the house,
between the bedroom window and the street lamp, is a tall tree, the
shadow of which is cast on to the bedroom wall in front of you.
There is a slight wind: the branches of the tree move, the shadows
of the branches move on the wall. Insects and small bats are flying
around the street lamp. The point of the example is obvious: the
relative movement of the shadows on the wall cannot, of itself,
offer us information about exactly what is happening outside the
window. Shadows of branches pass through shadows of branches,
shadows of fluttering moths and flitting bats move rapidly over the
wall, in and out of the branches. Shadow-bats and shadow-moths
are fluttering around the branches of the shadow-tree; they grow
larger and smaller as they move, they darken and they fade. The
real moths and real bats are flying around the street lamp, not the
tree. Knowing how things are in the world outside the window, we
know why the moths seem to grow larger and smaller as they flutter
amongst the branches: they are coming nearer and going further
away as they flutter round the lamp. If all the knowledge we had
was restricted to the play of shadows on the wall, we should have
a thoroughly fuddled picture of the relations between the moths
and the tree.

The relations amongst things, causal relations and spatial

relations especially, are not always manifest in the relations amongst reflections or shadows of things. The shadow-pattern has a complex projective relationship to the pattern of the real things. Once we know the pattern of the real things we can interpret the shadow-pattern: if we know no more than the shadow-pattern we are in a realm of illusory and potentially deceptive appearances and of ungroundable conjecture.

Plato's third image presents a vivid allegorical picture of the ascent from the realm of mere shadows to the final attainment of the intellectual intuition of the Good itself.

We are to imagine a vast cavern in which men have been imprisoned since childhood, chained neck and limb so that they can only gaze straight ahead. Behind and above the prisoners a fire burns, and between the fire and the prisoners lies a pathway with a wall beside it which screens the body of anyone moving along the pathway.

People move to and fro along the pathway carrying all sorts of objects including images of human beings and animals. Some of them talk to each other as they move to and fro. The firelight casts the shadows of the objects carried along the pathway on to the cavern wall in front of the prisoners. The prisoners, having nothing other to look at save the flickering shadows on the wall, see them as realities; the voices and sounds reflected from the cave wall they interpret as proceeding from the shadow-figures.

A prisoner released from his familiar chains and turned around to face the wall, the pathway, and the moving figures would be dazzled for a while, and then come to realize that the shadow-forms, which all his life he had taken for real things, were no more than mere illusions compared with the things he now sees.

Initially he would find the objects carried by difficult to identify: familiarity with the world of shadows has not prepared him to recognize the things which cast the shadows. The fire itself would hurt his eyes.

If the prisoner were then forced outside into the sunlight, he would at first be overcome by the splendour of the light and would need time to accustom himself to the light before he could look at things in the external world. At first he would find it easier to perceive shadows, reflections in water, and only then real objects.

At last he would be able to gaze directly at the sun and see the power which controls the visible world, which orders the seasons.

If such a man were then to return to the cavern and to resume his place amongst the chained prisoners, he would find he had lost his ability to discriminate the fine detail of the shadowplay on the cavern wall, he would be blinded by darkness, and seem to his companions an incompetent fool.

The image of the Cave represents the ascent of the mind from a realm of mere images to the realm of visible things (the objects carried along in the pathway and those who carry them) to the world of Forms (the objects in the external world) and finally to the intuition of the Good (the Sun).

There is a widespread doubt amongst Plato scholars as to the degree to which the image of the Cave can be mapped on to the image of the Line. The main problem in reconciling the two images concerns the interpretation of the chained prisoners. If their state is an image of *eikasia*, fuddled opinions based on reflections, shadows, and suchlike images, then we are forced to conclude that Socrates is here arguing that this is the normal state of the uneducated human being. This conclusion is difficult to accept; it seems to give shadows, reflections, and suchlike images an importance in human experience quite out of keeping with what common sense would allow. When was our experience of the world limited to the perception of reflection, shadows, and images? Even if we extend the class of objects of cognition in question to include echoes, marks, traces, and so forth, there seems to be no stage of human existence when our cognitive range is limited to images, shadows, echoes, and traces.

A modern reader attempting to come to terms with Plato's text will probably think of reflections and shadows primarily in terms of their derivative and dependent status. We take for granted the silvered-glass mirrors which are to be found in almost every room of every house. We take for granted the lifelike perfection of the reflection in a silvered-glass mirror. So common are such mirrors that they provide our normative image of a reflection. In Plato's day mirrors were made of polished hammered metal: such mirrors give a reflection far less perfect than that given by a mirror of silvered glass. A bronze mirror provides a vague and somewhat distorted image.

A modern reader of Plato takes for granted lamps which provide a brilliant steady light and cast sharply defined shadows. Plato's Athens had no gas lamps, no electric light bulbs: its indoor lighting was provided by burning wicks, flames that cast dim, flickering shadows. The sun, of course, casts sharp, clear shadows, but the shadows Plato has in mind in the Cave image are the flickering forms cast by firelight.

A modern reader thinks of reflections, shadows, and images mainly in terms of their derivative and dependent status. Such an emphasis may well lead us to misinterpret the force of Plato's Divided Line. To a reader of Plato's own day, reflections and shadows would almost certainly carry immediate and foregrounded associations of distortion and dimness which would not automatically occur to a modern reader.

If Plato is thinking of reflections, shadows, and suchlike images primarily in terms of their being generally distorted, vague, dim, indistinct, and flickering, then it may be possible to interpret the chained prisoners in such a way as to preserve a strict correspondence between the Divided Line and the Cave. That this is indeed the way he thinks is strongly suggested by the implication made in the image of the Divided Line that there is a difference in degree of clarity between our cognition of animals, plants, and artefacts and of images and reflections of them analogous to the difference in clarity between our cognition of intelligible things and of visible things.

In the *Phaedo* Socrates was made to argue that pleasure and pain are particularly dangerous in that they have a capacity to obsess the mind and to give us a completely distorted perception of things. The distinction between *eikasia* and *pistis* (and analogously the distinction between *dianoia* and *noesis*) is one of degree of clarity and obscurity. Under the dominance of pleasure and pain our cognition of things is distorted, lacking in clarity. In the stage of life before education has established harmonious order amongst the parts of the soul, and subordinated appetite to the governance of reason, human beings live under the dominance of appetite, enslaved to pleasure and pain. What state of cognition is attainable by a person whose perception of reality is distorted by the obsessive power of pleasure and pain? A person enslaved to the body's wants will scarcely apply himself to the intellectual discipline required of a scientist or a philosopher; it is incredible that he should attain to *dianoia* or to *noesis*. It is not evident such a person could even attain *pistis*.

Imagine two children: Cleon is the spoiled son of a wealthy family, Sophia the daughter of family of modest means and frugal lifestyle. Cleon has been brought up from babyhood by indulgent parents who pander to his every whim, Sophia by parents who ensure all her needs are provided for, but who educate her carefully in virtuous conduct, teaching her the simple truths about the world her childish mind is capable of appropriating. For Cleon the world of his experience is a field of pleasures: his appetites dominate his life, everything he sees, hears, touches, tastes, smells means and matters to him as a means or as an obstacle to his self-gratification. Sophia looks to the world about her for the fulfilment of her needs, but beyond that she approaches it with intellectual curiosity, seeking to learn, enjoying new discoveries rather than seeking sensuous pleasures.

Cleon's perception of the world is radically distorted; Sophia, even as a child, has acquired the kind of attitude to life which enables her to form sound opinions. Sophia can attain true *pistis*, Cleon is not likely to do so. He is trapped in *eikasia*, in a fuddled perception of a reality reflected in the distorting mirror of his pleasure-hungry soul.

The chained prisoners are, I would suggest, human beings in that state of slavery to pleasure and pain that is our common lot until an educative influence arouses an intellectual curiosity in us, and a readiness for self-restraint. Their state of cognition is *eikasia*, not because they spend their lives staring at mirrors and portraits, but because their perception of reality is distorted by their obsessive interest in pleasure and pain.

Education consists not in giving knowledge to those who lack it, as is commonly supposed: that, says Socrates, is as possible as putting sight into blind eyes. Education consists in turning peoples' minds from images to realities, from the sensuous world of perpetual flux to the stable world of intelligible realities, the realm of the Forms. Education does not endow a person with an intellectual capacity he did not formerly possess, it directs his intellect to the right objects. It is not giving sight to the blind, it is drawing the sighted away from the realm of flickering shadows to use their sight as it should be used, in the sunlit world of real things.

Society needs men and women who see things as they are. Minds which have ascended to knowledge of the Forms in the light of the Good will be tempted to remain for ever in the contemplation of intelligible reality. If society is to be governed by laws which embody the authentic principles of justice, then it needs lawmakers who have attained the knowledge of the Good, who understand the nature of Justice Itself. Such a lawmaker would have to be a person who has ascended to the intuition of the Good, but who returns to the world of political action in order to design the laws which will enable a just society to be established. The Ideal State will train its lawgivers in philosophy, so that they will know how to maintain order and unity in the state, governing it in such a way as to promote the welfare of all.

In the early dialogues Socrates furnishes us with a model of the philosopher as the truth-hunter, who subjects every opinion and every definition to the destructive testing of systematic dialectical questioning. The *Phaedo* presents the philosopher as an intellectual contemplative, who frees himself from the influence of the body in order to ascend to knowledge of the Forms. In the *Symposium* the true philosopher appears as the lover of beauty, who ascends by the power of his *eros* to rapturous vision of Beauty Itself. The philosopher of the *Republic* is both the intellectual contemplative of the *Phaedo* and the lover of truth and beauty of the *Symposium*; but here he is more: he is also the enlightened lawgiver, who returns from contemplation of the Good to involve himself in the practical political concerns of social life, to bring about rule of justice, to shape and form society so that the welfare of all is promoted. The philosopher's return to political involvement may be reluctant, but such a return is his duty if Justice is ever to be established on earth.

11

Problems with the Ideas: the *Parmenides*

The discussions in the *Phaedo*, *Symposium*, *Republic*, and *Phaedrus* are wide-ranging in subject-matter and varied in tone. None the less, these great dialogues of Plato's middle period present a coherent body of philosophical investigations. They are held together by Plato's conviction that beyond the shifting transient patterns of appearances which sense-experience furnishes there is an eternal, immutable, intelligible reality, knowledge of which can be attained through mathematical and dialectical reasoning. Intelligible reality consists of an ordered hierarchy of Forms or Ideas at the summit of which stands the Idea of the Good, the source of the existence and the intelligibility of the other Forms. The Forms are the source of the reality, the nature, the intelligibility, and the value of the various classes of sense-perceptible things. It is his understanding of these eternal Ideas which Plato believes allows him to attain the range of philosophical insights into human psychology, political and ethical theory, aesthetics, metaphysics, and epistemology which he presents in the dialogues.

What exactly the Ideas are, however, remains a question. They are eternal, unchangeable, immaterial, intelligible; they are the true objects of knowledge, the ultimate source of the reality, attributes, and value of all sensible things. That tells us the basic functions they perform in Plato's metaphysical and epistemological theories: it does not tell us what they are.

Knowing the importance of the Pythagorean influence on Plato, and noting the importance of mathematics in the programme of education designed to lead to knowledge of the Forms, we may be led to suspect they are mathematical realities of some kind. There is, however, nothing in the text of the *Phaedo* or the *Republic* to force us to such a conclusion, and we might come to quite a different view, for example that the Forms are eternal archetypes or paradigms of sense-perceptible things.

We know from the dialogues of Plato's middle period that some kind of hierarchy exists amongst the Ideas, and that they stand in some sort of relation to each other. At the summit of the intelligible realm stands the Idea of the Good, and we may conclude from the parallel between the pathway to knowledge of the Good in the *Republic* and the pathway to perception of Beauty Itself in the *Symposium* that the Idea of the Good is also, or somehow comprehends or subsumes, the Idea of Beauty, or is itself comprehended in or subsumed by the Idea of Beauty. We have been told that other Forms owe their existence and their intelligibility to this supreme Form: beyond that we know little of the order and structure of the Intelligible Realm.

In the *Parmenides* Socrates is presented as a young man, filled with enthusiasm for his Theory of Ideas, facing a series of sharp dialectical criticisms from Parmenides. Plato's use of Parmenides as a character in the dialogue has no historical significance; it has, however, considerable literary and philosophical significance. Plato's treatment of Parmenides is affectionate and respectful. He is reverenced for his dialectical skill and for his uncompromising intellectualism. The dialogue portrays Parmenides as a mature dialectician confronting a youthful Socrates whose presentation of the Theory of Ideas he subjects to rigorous criticism, using against Socrates the very techniques of continual systematic questioning which Socrates himself habitually uses in the early dialogues.

The cogency of Parmenides' criticisms of the Theory of Ideas have led some commentators to the conclusion that this dialogue signifies Plato's abandonment of the theory. Such an interpretation is quite unnecessary, and would leave us facing an historical absurdity, namely, either that Aristotle, despite all the nineteen years he spent in the Academy, never realized that Plato had given up the Theory of Forms, or that, knowing that Plato had abandoned the theory, he none the less felt it necessary to spend two entire books of the *Metaphysics* refuting it. There is no ancient evidence in favour of the view that Plato abandoned the Theory of Ideas.

Parmenides' criticisms are cogent, but they do not demolish

the whole of the Theory of Forms, rather they help clarify it. He identifies an array of problems central to the credibility of the theory and rejects certain ways of talking about the Ideas which are familiar from the *Phaedo* and the *Republic*. Parmenides' arguments promote the constructive reappraisal of the Theory of Ideas, not its abandonment. Inconsistencies and inadequacies are identified and removed, problems still remaining are clarified. The *Parmenides* may well represent the developing in Plato's thought of a clearer sense of the logical significance of the Forms. Hitherto his approach to them and his use of them has been from the standpoint of metaphysical and epistemological theory; the arguments of the *Parmenides* suggest a new interest in the Forms from the point of view of the theory of meaning and the problem of universals.

Parmenides argues:

1. If there are Ideas, then there is an Idea corresponding to every general term

The young Socrates is represented as confident in the existence of Forms of abstract values, Goodness, Beauty, Justice, and of mathematical realities and relations: Parmenides insists that the arguments which establish the existence of the Forms Socrates accepts also demonstrate that there are Forms of man, of fire, of water, hair, mud, and dirt. The implication of this is that there is a Form corresponding to every general term in the language, and a Form corresponding to every class.

Plato's writings do not contain any systematic set of arguments for the existence of the Forms. It is none the less certain that a set of such arguments was known and studied in the Academy. In the *Metaphysics* Aristotle refers to a number of arguments for the existence of the Forms without explaining what exactly the arguments are; he evidently assumed that the students listening to him were familiar with the arguments.

None of the ways in which we demonstrate the existence of Forms actually works. Some do not necessarily produce that conclusion; from some there proceed Forms of things of which we hold there are none. For according to the arguments from the sciences there are Forms of all things of which there are sciences, according to the 'one-over-many' argument even of negations, according to that from knowledge of what has passed away of perishables, since we have some mental image of such things. Even the most exact arguments produce, in the one case Ideas of relations, of which we hold there is no substantive class, and in the other the 'Third Man' (990 b).

Aristotle does not lay out the arguments mentioned. The commentator Alexander does, and may well have had before him a now lost work of Aristotle on the Ideas. Unfortunately we are not certain that Alexander's account is accurate; it could well have been influenced by later Platonist arguments. Even so, it is possible to reconstruct the arguments to which Aristotle refers with a modest degree of certainty.

(a) 'from the sciences'

The objects studied by the sciences, a Platonist would argue, are not merely individual entities, their attributes and relations, and the processes in which they are involved: the sciences study the patterns and structures underlying and instantiated in the world of sense-experience. The sciences require as their objects fixed, permanent realities, not transient, shifting appearances. If the sciences have any validity, if they can attain knowledge, then there must be a realm of immutable, intelligible realities which are the true objects of the sciences.

The argument from the sciences leads us from the fact that there exist sciences to the conclusion that there must exist objects of the sciences which are of such a kind as to make scientific enquiry a meaningful activity and to provide an adequate ground for scientific knowledge. If the objects of our cognition were limited to the things given in sense-experience, then science would collapse into a mere chronicling of the shifting, changing patterns of appearances.

(b) 'the one over many'

Consider any general term which can be applied to a number of different things, such as 'man'. Socrates is a man; Alcibiades is a man. The predicate 'man', however, is not exhausted by its instances. Socrates and Alcibiades are instances of man, but neither is identical with what the term 'man' names; its range of reference extends beyond any specific subject of which it is predicable, even beyond the totality of subjects of which at any given time it is predicable. Socrates and Alcibiades, Hippias, Callias, and Euthyphro are all instances of man; in their multiplicity they are none the less a unity in virtue of their common man-ness. But that unity is not in them as individuals nor even as a collectivity; it transcends them. The unity of the collective class must be grounded in something beyond the individual members of the class, or even their collective totality. We are invited to conclude there is something which functions as the ground of unity of each class designated by a general term. Whatever this is, and for the Platonist it is a Form or Idea corresponding to the particular class, it will also be that to which the general term corresponding to the class refers, and at the same time the ground of meaning of the term.

(c) 'from knowledge of what has passed away'

Our knowledge of what it is to be a man is not affected by the passing away of any individual man or even of all the men that happen to exist at a particular moment in time. For the Platonist, identifying the true object of our knowledge with something transient would leave our knowledge ungrounded if that object ceased to exist. The object of our knowledge, then, is not the transient individual instance, nor is it any collection of such instances, it is the permanent reality of which those instances are instances, in the example under consideration, the Idea of Man.

(d) The argument which leads to Ideas of Relations

This argument is probably the one presented briefly in the *Phaedo*.

We see two pieces of wood as equal, but at the same time recognize their equality is imperfect. All instances of equality are imperfect; how then could any or all of them be the source of our concept of equality? How indeed do we recognize the relative and impermanent equality of the pieces of wood? The Platonist would argue that we require knowledge of Equality itself, the perfect Form of equality, in order to recognize the imperfect instances as, despite their imperfection, instances of equality.

It is worth commenting on this argument that, since the Idea of Equality is one Plato himself introduces in the *Phaedo*, the anxiety which seems now to attend the notion of there being Ideas of relations must have emerged at some later point in Plato's intellectual development.

(e) The argument which leads to the 'Third Man'

When different things share the same name they do so in virtue of there being something to which the common name refers. The Platonist accounts for the way in which the name 'man' for example is applied to Socrates, Callias, and Crito by reference to their participation in Man-ness, the Idea of Man. The name 'man' refers primarily not to the transient individuals who also bear it but to the eternal Idea by participation in which the individual man is a man, and is called 'man'.

If the arguments for the existence of the Forms current in the Academy were indeed those indicated by Aristotle, then they do seem to have had the generality of application Parmenides' first argument would require. Aristotle himself does not criticize the arguments for any lack of generality: he attacks their logical inadequacies and their tendency to prove, if anything, too much. Perhaps the *Parmenides* represents a turning-point in Plato's own intellectual development at which, having realized and taken on board the fuller implications of the arguments by which the existence of the Forms was established, he engages in a self-critical review of the theory, removing the inconsistencies and abandoning aspects of the theory which cannot withstand rigorous logical criticism.

2. If the whole Idea is present in each of its instances then the Idea exists separate from itself. If only a part of the Idea is present in each instance then the Idea is divisible

One of the greatest difficulties Plato faces in constructing an adequate Theory of Ideas, is that of explaining how it is that the particular instances of X participate in the Idea of X-ness. This second argument of Parmenides is directed against accounts of participation which would make the Forms actually present in particulars which instantiate them.

The force of the arguments is considerable: if the entire Idea of Mountain is present in Kilimanjaro and the entire Idea of Mountain is present in Kanchenjunga, then the Idea of Mountain is separated from itself by several thousand miles. If only part of the Idea of Mountain is present in Kilimanjaro and a different part of the Idea is present in Kanchenjunga, then quite absurd consequences follow: are we to admit there is nothing in common in the ways in which they are mountains, has the Idea of Mountain become reduced to a small fragment in each?

Socrates makes the interesting suggestion that the Form could be totally present in every instance as Day is present in many places and is yet one: Parmenides argues that Socrates' analogy has no more plausibility than the claim that a huge sail spread over many persons is above each person in its entirety. Socrates' suggestion can survive Parmenides' attack: Parmenides is right that in reality only a part of the sail is over the head of each individual person: that does not entail that only part of the day is in any given place. If it is morning in Manchester and morning in London it does not follow that one part of the morning is in Manchester and another part is in London. It is at least possible that Plato is trailing an evident fallacy to suggest a way out of the problem.

It is important to realize that these objections are not frivolous. Any solution to the problem of the meaning and reference of general terms has to avoid implying that whatever it is that is common to the various individuals which share a particular name is actually present, wholly or partly, in the individuals in such a way as to give rise to absurd conclusions of the kind indicated.

3. If in the many things which are Z we recognize the Idea of Z-ness, then, if we consider the Idea of Z together with the many individual Zs there must be another Idea of Z-ness in virtue of which the Idea of Z and the individual Zs are all Z

This argument is famous from Aristotle's use of it: he calls it the argument of the 'Third Man'. The specific example Parmenides uses is the Form of Bigness: if the Form of Bigness is itself big then, since the name 'big' is a common term applying to all those things that are big because they participate in the Form of Bigness, and also to the Form of Bigness itself, there must of necessity be another Form of Bigness in virtue of which they are all big and are all called 'big'. This argument leads inevitably to an infinite regress. Not only does it establish a second Form of Bigness: if that too is admitted to be big, then another and another and another Form must be supposed to exist, until we end up accounting for the bigness of things that are big by asserting the existence of an infinite hierarchy of Forms of Bigness.

If the Theory of Ideas is to escape from the Third Man argument, then we must avoid any implication that the Idea of Z-ness is itself an instance of Z-ness in the same sense that an individual Z is. There seems no difficulty in admitting that the Form of Table is not itself a table or that the Form of Man is not itself a man, but it seems difficult to accept that the Form of Good is not itself good. Plato can escape the Third Man argument and yet accept that in some cases at least the Form of Z-ness is itself Z, provided he can furnish an account of the ways in which 'Z' is predicated of the Form of Z-ness which distinguishes it from the way in which 'Z' is predicated of the individual instances of Z-ness. Aristotle's analyses of the ways in which terms have meaning seems to provide us with the basis for just such an account. He discusses how the term 'healthy' is predicated of various subjects:

> a living creature is called 'healthy' because of the presence of health in it
> a diet is called 'healthy' because it causes health
> a complexion is called 'healthy' because it signifies health.

This form of predication Aristotle calls predication 'from one and to one'; in much later centuries it was renamed 'Analogy of Attribution'. Analogy of attribution occurs when the same term (such as 'healthy') is predicated of a number of different subjects (such as Socrates, his diet, his complexion) in virtue of the different relations in which they stand to something (in this case, health).

In its primary sense, 'healthy' = 'possessing health',
in secondary senses, 'healthy' = 'causing health' or
'signifying health'.

Aristotle himself does not discuss what relevance his model of
predication from-one-and-to-one might have to the analysis of
the way in which we talk of the Platonic Ideas. None the less, his
model suggests a way out of the Third Man argument.

Let us take the Form of Beauty as a test case. What is required
if we are to escape from the Third Man argument is an analysis
of the statement 'The Form of Beauty is beautiful' which does
not commit us to including the Form of Beauty in a class of
beautifuls with other instances of beauty—for example, Alcibiades and Charmides. If we say:

Alcibiades is beautiful and
The Form of Beauty is beautiful

then the model of Analogy of Attribution allows us to move to
the following analysis:

Alcibiades possesses beauty
The Form of Beauty causes beauty

The analysis escapes the Third Man argument, but in an unsatisfactory way. To analyse 'The Form of Beauty is beautiful'
as 'The Form of Beauty causes beauty' is inadequate. Certainly
Plato would wish to claim that the Form of Beauty causes beauty
to exist in all beautiful things, but that is not the only sense in
which the Form of Beauty is beautiful. An analogy will make this
clear: if we use the term 'hot' according to Analogy of Attribution, then we can say 'This match is hot', since the match causes
heat when struck. If the Form of Beauty is beautiful only in the
sense that a match is hot, then the beauty of the Form of Beauty
seems to have been analysed away.

A different analysis is needed. The Form of Beauty is not only
the cause of beauty in Alcibiades and Charmides, it is also Beauty
Itself. The Form of Beauty does not only cause beauty, it *is*
Beauty: it is that transcendent, eternal, unchanging Beauty in
which Alcibiades and Charmides participate for a while and in
virtue of which they are beautiful.

The Form of Beauty is beautiful = The Form of Beauty is Beauty

Alcibiades is beautiful = Alcibiades participates in Beauty

Here we seem to have an analysis which preserves Plato's doctrine, avoids the Third Man argument, and makes perfectly good sense.

4. If the Forms are mental concepts, then, since everything participates in the Forms, everything consists of thoughts

If we accept that there are Forms and that all sensible particulars exist by participation in the Forms, then we cannot accept that Forms are merely concepts or ideas in the mind. Tempting as such a reductionist view might be, it would leave us with a world consisting solely of thoughts; if things are what they are by participation in the Ideas, and if the Ideas are mental contents, then there seems no way in which things could be other than mental contents. The Forms are not concepts or thoughts, they are objects of thought. Without the Forms thought would have no objects and no content.

5. If the Forms are paradigms in which things participate by imitating them, the Theory of Forms is liable to infinite regress

If the Forms are patterns or paradigms and if their instances participate in them by resemblance or imitation, then the Theory of Forms will be unable to escape from the Third Man or a similar argument.

This criticism seems to liquidate some aspects of the Theory of Forms as Plato himself proposes it in the *Republic*. In his discussion of how a craftsman makes a bed, for example, Plato seems to imply that the Idea of Bed is a pattern which the craftsman follows, and to suggest precisely the kind of interpretation of the Ideas Parmenides refutes.

6. If the Forms are totally separate from our world, then we can have no knowledge of them

Plato always faces the problem of explaining how exactly we can be led from our immersion in the world of sense-experience to becoming aware of the Forms. In the *Meno* we were shown how systematic questioning can clear away false opinion and lead to a bewildered ignorance, which further questioning can lead to recollection of a reality known before birth. In the *Phaedo* we are shown how an imperfect instance of, for example, equality can help reawaken our recollection of the perfect Form of which it is an instance. In the *Symposium* and the *Phaedrus* the special function of Beauty is to lead us beyond the world of sense-perceptible things to awareness of the Forms, since beauty is the most manifest of the Forms, and since we have a psychological need for Beauty. If the Forms exist totally separate from the world of our experience, then the path of ascent from the world of the senses to the Forms is no longer merely difficult, it does not exist. The gods may know the Forms; we have no longer any means of doing so.

Parmenides' arguments have laid down the conditions an adequate Theory of Ideas must meet: it must be a totally general theory, it must avoid any account of the participation of particulars in the Ideas which leads to the division of the Ideas or the existence of an Idea in several distinct places at once, it must avoid the Third Man paradox and must not reduce Ideas to mere concepts or to paradigms. It is quite clear that much of what Plato himself has said about the Ideas in the *Phaedo* and the *Republic* cannot stand the criticism of the *Parmenides*. In Book I of the *Metaphysics* Aristotle accuses Plato of making a merely verbal shift in speaking of 'participation' rather than 'imitation': this is now visible as a serious challenge to the credibility of the Theory of Ideas. Any talk of the Ideas as patterns or paradigms, of participation as the presence of the Ideas in particulars or as resemblance or imitation is now to be treated with extreme suspicion.

12

The nature of knowledge: the *Theaetetus*

The *Parmenides* shows Plato engaged with serious difficulties which flow not only from misunderstandings of the theory of Forms, but even from his own formulation of that theory as it is presented to the reader in the *Phaedo*, the *Symposium*, and the *Republic*. It shows also a shifting of focus in Plato's discussion of the Forms towards the central logical questions relating to the theory. The *Theaetetus*, deservedly one of the best known of Plato's dialogues, focuses on the central epistemological question of the nature of knowledge: whereas in the *Meno* the theory of Recollection has been proposed to account for how we know, and in the *Phaedo* and the *Republic* the theory of Forms or Ideas has been presented as identifying the objects of knowledge, what we know, the *Theaetetus* focuses directly on the question of the nature of knowledge—not its content or objects, nor the means by which we acquire it, but what knowledge is.

The *Theaetetus* was probably composed about the same period as the *Parmenides*, perhaps some twenty years before Plato's death. Since we know that Aristotle studied in the Academy for nineteen years, the dialogues of the period of the *Theaetetus* should offer us some indication of the questions under discussion in the Academy when he first became a student there. They may contain reflections of the impact Aristotle's particular style of philosophical mentality had on Plato himself, though this is a matter of speculation since we lack the evidence to determine what part, if any, Aristotle played in the development of Plato's philosophical investigations.

Theaetetus, the principal speaker in the dialogue other than Socrates himself, is a young mathematician commended to Socrates' attention by his teacher Theodorus. Socrates engages the young man in conversation and questions him in his familiar manner to test the truth of the fine report Theodorus has given of his intellectual abilities. After a preliminary exchange, Socrates shapes the conversation towards the question of the nature of knowledge. Theaetetus falls into the familiar trap of offering a list of examples instead of a definition. When Socrates points out to him that what he is asking is not what kinds of knowledge there are, but what knowledge itself is, Theaetetus is quick to grasp the point Socrates is making. He shows how well he understands by relating to Socrates how he and his friend, Socrates' namesake the young Socrates, had been involved in classifying and defining real and surd roots of numbers. 'Come then,' says Socrates (148 d), 'you have made a fine start just now. Take your own answer about roots as a model; just as you encompassed them all within one class, try to bring the different kinds of knowledge under a single definition.' Theaetetus demurs; he has often made such an attempt, he says, when he has heard reports of the questions Socrates asks, but he feels no confidence in his own ability to answer well, nor does he know of anyone else capable of satisfying Socrates with his answers. 'It makes me feel apprehensive!' he says. 'These are labour-pains, my dear Theaetetus,' Socrates answers, 'you are not empty, but pregnant!'

Socrates now develops an image of himself as an intellectual midwife, helping young men bring their ideas to birth, and then discerning whether the new-born idea is genuine or a mere sham, an empty image or genuine thought:

I am not at all wise, myself; I have no discovery or mental offspring of my own to display, but people who associate with me, though at first some of them seem quite dull, as we get to know each other better, then, if God is good to them, they progress remarkably, not just in their own eyes but in others' as well. It is certain they never learn anything from me, the many splendid things they discover and bring to birth are from themselves. But they do owe the delivery of them to God and to me. (150 d)

Socrates does not, he says, convey knowledge to his associates; his question-games enable them to form their ideas and bring them to expression so that a judgement can be made of their quality. Some of his associates, having abandoned his ministrations too precipitately, either looking down on Socrates or falling under the influence of others, have failed to nurture and develop their intellectual progeny in the right way, and have ended up making fools of themselves. Some have seen what has happened to them, and have returned begging to be taken back into Socrates' society and to submit once again to his treatment. Others have come to him barren and he has acted the role of intellectual marriage-broker, introducing them to the person who will provide the effective cure for their intellectual sterility: he mentions Prodicus in particular as a person to whom he has sent many students.

The image of the midwife captures vividly the positive educational function of the Socratic dialectic: by questioning the position an interlocutor takes up Socrates tests it for consistency and coherence, clarifies it, and enables its implications to emerge. As it is presented in the text the image is an image of Socrates; to what extent it is intended to apply more widely as an image of what the philosopher should be as educator we are left to speculate.

The examination of the three definitions of knowledge successively advanced by Theaetetus is lengthy and complex and some parts of it are difficult for a modern reader to follow. None the less, the principal arguments of the *Theaetetus* remain of great philosophical interest and significance; the main issues of the dialogue have had a determining influence on the agenda of centuries of epistemological debate. The discussions of knowledge and belief in the *Meno* and the *Republic* contrast knowledge and belief as distinct cognitive states. In the *Meno* we move from true belief to knowledge by grounding true belief, by mining out what it is that makes the belief true, what from a metaphysical point of view would constitute the causal ground of what we correctly believe to be the case. In the *Republic* belief and knowledge have different epistemological bases and distinct objects: true belief is based in awareness of the world of sense-experience, material perceptible things; knowledge has the Forms as its object. This need not imply that the same proposition cannot be believed at one point or by one person and at another point or to another person represent something known: it is not the linguistic or logical formulation of propositions which interests Plato in the central books of the *Republic*, it is rather the metaphysical grounding of knowledge in the intuition of an eternal and intelligible object-matter. Indeed one of the major oddities which faces a modern reader of the epistemological discussions in the *Republic* is the degree to which the statements or propositions we may claim to know or believe are ignored in the account Plato offers of the nature of knowledge and belief.

In response to Socrates' questioning, Theaetetus proffers three successive attempted definitions of knowledge:

(*a*) knowledge is nothing but sense-perception (151 e)
(*b*) knowledge is true belief (187 b)
(*c*) knowledge is true belief plus a *logos* (rationale, explanation, account?) (201 c–d)

(*a*) Knowledge is perception

'In my opinion anyone who knows something perceives that which he knows, and so, as it seems at the moment, knowledge is nothing other than perception.' Socrates congratulates Theaetetus on his attempted definition, which he identifies with Protagoras' claim that 'man is the measure of all things, of those that exist that they exist and of those that do not exist that they do not exist'. This both Theaetetus and Socrates interpret to imply that whatever an individual person perceives at any given moment is real for him at that moment. Socrates weaves that claim together with an account of the world of experience that sees the whole sensible world as a complex of patterns of motion, the specific sense-experiences of an individual being constituted in and by the interplay of various motions including those which are his sense-organs.

Socrates demonstrates how different states of the perceiver can lead to an object of perception appearing, and therefore, for him, being different from what they would otherwise be. When I am well the same wine is sweet and wholesome that is bitter to me when I am ill. The different qualities the wine has for me at different times are equally real to me. Given that my perceptions are always true for me, then the identification of perception and knowledge which Theaetetus has proposed seems quite credible.

Having so far approached Theaetetus' attempted definition with sympathy, attempting to bring his thought to birth in its fullness, Socrates now raises a series of objections to test the definition's soundness. Why should it only be man, he asks, who is the measure of all things, why not a pig, a baboon, or even a tadpole? The argument is not frivolous: if the human being's perceptions are real for him, there seems no reason to deny that the pig's perceptions are equally real to the pig, and the baboon's perceptions to the baboon. Equally, the objection does not necessarily embarrass a defender of Protagoras; the claim that the individual human being is the judge of reality in the sense that he or she is the only person in a position to experience what he or she experiences, need not necessarily exclude the pig and even the tadpole from sharing the same privilege to the degree that they too actually have experience. It is possible to defend the Protagorean formulation as it stands only if it is possible to argue that the human being's perceptions differ from those of the pig and the baboon to such an extent that the latter cannot seriously be thought of as having a cognitive content. An alternative argument which located the significant difference between the human being and the baboon in the possession, or lack, of a capacity to form rational judgements about what is given in perception, or of a capacity to use language would undermine the very position it sought to defend, by introducing a distinction between perception and judgement which would call in question the identification of knowledge with perception.

Socrates proposes a more serious objection: if everything is for each person as he perceives it, if each person is the sole judge and indeed the infallible judge of how things are for him, then there seems to be no justification for any claim to judge the accuracy of another person's perceptions or the truth of the statements he makes about them. What then are we to make of the claims of the professional teacher such as Protagoras himself? His own doctrine seems to undermine his professional claims.

It is possible for Protagoras to answer this objection too: he must, of course, refrain from the claim to teach truth to those who are in error, but he can reasonably claim that, although each person's perceptions are equally true, they are not equally worthwhile. Socrates himself advances this answer on Protagoras' behalf. It is possible, for example, to wish a person to replace the perceptions he or she has in a state of sickness with those he would have in a healthy state, not because the latter are more true or more real, but because they are more useful. Protagoras' work as a teacher is, in this interpretation, akin to the work of the doctor, developing and promoting health rather than offering instruction or purveying wisdom.

Socrates continues to undermine the Protagorean thesis by offering Theaetetus a suggestive example: when we see or hear words of a foreign language we do not understand; we have to admit we perceive what is written here, or what such a one has said, but if perception is identical with knowledge, then it must follow that we also know what is written here, that we know what such a one has said. Theaetetus' careful response gives away more than he would wish:

We shall aver, Socrates, that we know of them exactly that which we see and hear: in the one case it is their colour and form that we see and know, in the other case the high and low pitch is what we hear and know: the things that grammarians and interpreters teach about them we do not perceive by sight or hearing, nor do we know them. (163 b–c)

Theaetetus' response distinguishes sharply between what of language is actually given in visual and auditory perception, and is therefore according to his own definition also known, namely the colours and shapes of written words, the sound-qualities, pitch, duration, and so forth in the case of speech, and what is not given in perception and therefore not known, for example meaning. What Theaetetus may not realize is that this distinction opens up a significant place in cognition for interpretation, opinion, and judgement.

Socrates proposes a further objection: if a man sees an object, then by Theaetetus' definition, he knows it. If he shuts his eyes, he may remember it, but he no longer perceives it: if knowledge and perception are identical, it then follows that he no longer knows it.

The most paradoxical of Socrates' objections is based directly on Protagoras' own words. He quotes Protagoras (170 a) as asserting that 'that which appears to a person actually is for him as it appears to be'. Everyone, says Socrates, believes himself wiser than others in some things, less wise in others. In a crisis we look for help to the expert, the person who excels us in knowledge. It is the common opinion that some are learned and wise, some ignorant. It is also the common view that 'wisdom is true reasoning and ignorance false opinion'. If, then, we are to follow Protagoras' own dictum that whatever appears actually is for the person as it appears, it must be the case that for the great majority of people wisdom is indeed true reasoning and the possession of some, ignorance false opinion and the state of others, and Protagoras' own opinion merely his own idiosyncratic reality. If, that is to say, Protagoras is right, then it follows that for most people he is wrong. Indeed, he is obliged by his own account to accept that those who believe his own view is false are correct in that belief!

Socrates now moves to develop the distinction between perception and judgement: it may well be the case that, as Protagoras asserts, a person's sense-perceptions really are for him as they appear to him to be; it does not follow that the same is true of his opinions and judgements. Even if a follower of Protagoras were to accept that whatever a given state believes to be just or unjust, honourable and dishonourable, is indeed so, it would be an extravagant and incredible conclusion to draw that whatever laws a state may frame to promote justice and honourable conduct will be equally expedient. No doubt the state always aims at establishing the most expedient laws; it is clear that it can fail in that aim. Judgements of what is expedient are judgements about what will happen in the future, what will result from a particular course of action rather than another possible course of action: even if Protagoras were right in asserting that man is the measure of what is, it does not follow he is the measure of what will be. It is one thing to attribute infallibility to perception, quite another to attribute it to prediction. In crucially important issues we look to an expert for predictions, a doctor to give a prognosis in illness, a cook to decide what dishes will make a dinner party a success.

The need for account to be taken of the role of judgement in cognition is emphasized in the final argument Socrates advances against Theaetetus' identification of knowledge and perception.

He points to the specialized functions of the bodily sense-organs; it is through the eye we perceive visual qualities, colours, and shapes, through the ear we perceive sounds, through the olfactory organ smells, and so forth. If we ask which organ enables us to make judgements that range across more than one field of sense-experience, we find no sense-organ that seems to carry this function. If we ask how it is we possess mathematical knowledge, or how we are able to make the judgement that two things are the same, or different from each other, there seems to be no bodily sense-organ through which such knowledge is attained, or which allows such judgements to be made. Theaetetus admits himself unable to defend his position against this argument:

THEAETETUS. You are referring to being and not-being, similarity and dissimilarity, identity and otherness, and unity too, and any other number applied to them. Your question evidently is through what bodily organs we mentally perceive odd and even and anything else of the same kind.

SOCRATES. Excellent, Theaetetus, you follow me. That is exactly my question.

THE. My goodness, Socrates, I have not a word to say, unless I hazard the opinion that there is no special organ for these things such as there is for those others [i.e. the sense qualities, colours, sound, etc.], it rather appears to me that the mind of itself discerns the universals in everything. (185 c–d)

Theaetetus has now accepted the crucial distinction at which several of Socrates' arguments have been aimed: the senses are the vehicles of our awareness of colours, shapes, sounds, smells, textures, heat, cold, and all the other sense-qualities; the fact that a thing exists or not, what essentially it is, its degree of resemblance to another is not something given through the senses; it has to be judged, reasoned out. As Socrates says (186 d), 'Knowledge is not constituted by sense impressions, but by the inferences we make about them; by that means being and truth are attainable, in the other way it is impossible.'

(b) Knowledge is true belief

Theaetetus' first attempted definition of knowledge cannot survive Socrates' attack. He now (187 b) proposes a second: 'It is impossible to say all opinion is knowledge, Socrates, since there is such a thing as false opinion. Perhaps knowledge is true opinion, let that be my answer. If this too is disproved as we go on, I'll have to try another!'

Socrates raises a number of objections. If we have an opinion about something, then presumably, he argues, we must know what we have an opinion about: how then can there be false opinion? Either we know what we know, and our opinions are true, or we lack knowledge, in which case we are in no position to make judgements or form opinions; our state would surely be that of ignorance, not false opinion. This argument is to all intents and purposes identical to one canvassed in the *Euthydemus*, and has gained nothing in plausibility since its earlier appearance. Equally unconvincing is Socrates' argument that false belief is belief in what is not, and that, since what is not is nothing, it is not thinkable; he who thinks what is not, thinks nothing, he does not think, and false belief is therefore impossible. This preposterous argument seems to have been something of a sophistical pot-boiler. It is hard to imagine that Plato intends these arguments to be taken very seriously; they seem little more than the intellectual equivalent of wire puzzles.

Socrates offers an alternative analysis of false opinion: each element of what we think or judge may well be something real, but in error we may put the bits together in the wrong way. Theaetetus is happy to accept this. Socrates now constructs a simple model of thinking or reasoning as 'the mind's conversing with itself about whatever it is considering' (189 e), questioning itself, responding, asserting, denying. When the mind eventually arrives at a decision on a given topic, that is what we regard as opinion: 'whenever anybody thinks something is something else, he is actually telling himself the one thing is the other'. This Socrates quickly develops into the absurd picture of someone telling himself the beautiful is ugly or the wrong right, or solemnly attempting to persuade himself that an ox is a horse or that one is two. This model of thought as the silent conversation of the soul with itself makes the idea of false opinion intelligible at the price of its being incredible that anyone should actually do what would be required for him reasonably to be said to hold a false opinion.

Not surprisingly Socrates is unwilling to persist in the paradoxical position in which his own arguments would leave him. He
constructs a new model of knowledge to evade the unacceptable
consequences to which he has led himself. He pictures the human
mind as containing a block of wax, which will differ in qualities in
different persons. He images remembering as our using the
mental wax to take an impression of the thing to be remembered.
Our memory of the thing lasts as long as the impression lasts; as
the impression fades, we forget. This model enables us to form
an idea of how false opinion can occur: when we make use of
memory in experience, it is possible to mismatch a memory-
impression with what is at any particular moment given in sense-
experience. It is just like putting the wrong shoe on the wrong
foot, he says. We differ in our ease of learning and in the readiness with which we forget what experience has impressed on the
wax of memory; we differ also in the degree of clarity and pre-
cision of the impression the wax can form.

One aim Socrates has had in constructing the wax-impression
model of memory is to avoid the paradox of claiming that the
existence of false belief would entail the person who falsely
believes something thinking one thing which he knows to be
another thing which he also knows. So long as we restrict the
cases in which false belief can arise to cases in which we are in
error in relating memory-impressions to the data of sense-
experience, the paradox does not arise. If, however, we are
prepared to accept the possibility of someone's making a simple
error in arithmetic (adding five and six, for example, and getting
twelve as the answer), then the paradox at once arises. The person
who makes the error knows what twelve is and knows what six is
and knows what five is; knowing the numbers he has none the less
told himself that the sum of five and six is twelve; he has con-
founded eleven and twelve, though he knows both. Knowing
both numbers and holding erroneous opinions about them, it
seems that he both knows and does not know one and the same
thing.

Socrates now advances another image; he distinguishes having
a thing from merely possessing it. He interprets possessing as a
lesser, more restricted kind of having: we might, for example,

possess a cloak but never actually use it, or possess a bird in a cage but be unable to grasp it. He now images the human mind as an aviary full of birds; some are gregarious creatures that flock together, others fly about the place alone or in little groups. The birds are the various kinds of knowledge we acquire. Originally the aviary of our mind was empty; as we grow and learn it acquires a population. The knower sometimes has a given bird in his hand, as it were; sometimes the same bird flies around free, available for recapture if we have the skill. The birds image the two senses in which I may be said to know something because I have learned it: in the one sense I possess the knowledge and under the right conditions and with the right skills I can bring that knowledge to hand, in the other I have the knowledge to hand, I have no need to hunt for it. This gives us a useful distinction between the mere possession of knowledge and having knowledge in such a way that it is immediately accessible and usable. Given this distinction, the paradoxicality of the error of the erring arithmetician is vapourized: he went looking for a pigeon in the aviary of his mind and grabbed a ring-dove instead.

At once, however, a new paradox is disclosed: the ring-dove and the pigeon are both bits of knowledge in the mental store-house; how can the grasping of a bit of knowledge constitute an error? Theaetetus' answer is immediate: perhaps we should see some of the birds in our cognitive aviary as error-birds; false belief would then rise not from catching the wrong knowledge-bird, but from taking hold of an error-bird.

This answer leads to yet a further paradox. The person who grasps hold of an error does so believing he has a piece of knowledge in his mental hand. If he can make that judgement, then he knows what knowledge is, and what error is, indeed he must be using his knowledge of what they are to distinguish between them even abstractly. In grasping an error-bird and taking it for a knowledge-bird, he is not knowing what he evidently knows. Solving this paradox by reapplying the aviary model at a second cognitive level is of limited value, since the paradox can be generated once again at a higher level; a progress to infinity would have started.

Socrates now moves to a quite different kind of argument. He lays aside the question of whether or not there can be false opinions and invites Theaetetus to consider what happens when those sitting in judgement in a lawcourt are persuaded to accept as true something which is indeed true, but which could only be known to be true by a witness: this example shows the contrast between knowledge and true belief.

(c) Knowledge is true belief plus a *logos*

Theaetetus responds to the distinction Socrates has made by repeating something he has heard from a source he cannot recall, that true belief combined with a *logos* is knowledge, true belief without a *logos* not knowledge. The term *logos* regularly poses problems for translators, not least here; it could mean 'reason' or 'explanation' or 'rationale' or 'account'. The implications of what follows in the dialogue seem to be in favour of reading it as referring to an explanatory rationale. What, then, Theaetetus is saying is that the mere possession of true belief does not of itself constitute knowledge; the knower must also possess an explanation or rationale which, conjoined with the true belief, will justify a claim to the possession of knowledge.

Socrates' immediate response is to engage in a lengthy argument directed to demonstrating the unintelligibility of the elementary letters of which syllables are composed, contrasting this with the claimed intelligibility of the syllables they compose. The point of this argument is, to say the least, not immediately obvious. It should probably be read as a pointer to a paradox of a particularly disturbing kind. If our model of understanding is based on the analysis of whatever it is that we are trying to understand into its ultimate elementary constituents, then we have a model that can only apply to complex realities and which terminates immediately we are face to face with the ultimate elements themselves. It is a trivially obvious tautology that the ultimate unanalysable elements of things cannot be understood by analysis. If our model of understanding is the analysis of what is to be understood into its ultimate elements, then we have to face the difficulty that the ultimate elements are themselves unintelligible; at best, the content of our understanding is a list of elements and the pattern of arrangement of the elements.

Socrates then proceeds to attack Theaetetus' third definition head-on. He offers three possible interpretations of what might be meant by a *logos*:

1. A verbal account mirroring the speaker's opinion

The problem with this definition is that anyone capable of the use of language will eventually be able to formulate his opinions in words which mirror them, but by this first definition he will then possess true belief plus a *logos* and therefore knowledge as well. Knowledge, in other words, would collapse into true belief, an identification which has already been rejected.

2. A systematic account of whatever is under discussion in terms of its elements

This initially more plausible suggestion generates an absurdity: suppose someone believes (correctly) that the name of Plato's teacher is spelled SOCRATES, and also believes (incorrectly) that the name of Socrates' wife is spelled ZANTIPPE. He possesses a true belief about the spelling of Socrates' name, and can offer an ordered account of its elements; it would, however, be a very brave claim that this constituted knowledge, since he may well just happen to be able to give such an account, just as he happens not to be able to give an ordered account of the elements of the name of Xanthippe. The name-speller himself may possess no criteria whatsoever to allow him to judge that his spelling of 'Socrates' is correct and his spelling of 'Xanthippe' erroneous; under such circumstances the claim that his mere ability to list the letters of Socrates' name is, of itself, sufficient to transform his true belief about how it is spelled into knowledge reduces knowledge to true belief plus a list that just happens to be right—knowledge by serendipity, and that is not what we mean by knowledge.

3. The ability to identify a characteristic which distinguishes the object in question from all others

This seems at first sight a little more hopeful; the *logos* is now not merely a statement of opinion or a list of parts, but a yardstick of correct identification. Unfortunately, Socrates quickly shows that this definition too masks an absurdity. He points out that having a right opinion about something already presupposes the ability to identify it; how could anyone be said to have a correct belief about something if it was impossible for him to identify what the belief is about? Once again knowledge collapses into true belief, which Socrates has already demonstrated is not knowledge.

Socrates has applied his art of midwifery to Theaetetus' attempted definitions of knowledge, and all three have turned out to be wind-eggs. We are left, as is he, without any satisfactory definition of knowledge. The dialogue has, of course, usefully eliminated a series of unsatisfactory candidates, but that is scarcely enough. We are left in that state of *aporia* which is the typical fruit of the dialectical questionings of the early dialogues, to which the *Theaetetus* now appears to bear a significant resemblance.

It is notable that the Forms or Ideas have made no appearance in the *Theaetetus*. Perhaps Plato has been making a serious attempt to put aside a theory with so many problems about it as the *Parmenides* shows to beset the Theory of Ideas. Perhaps, and more probably, we are meant to notice their absence and speculate as to whether the Ideas offer any way out of the impasse into which the *Theaetetus* has led us. Perhaps too we are intended to notice how relatively perfunctory is Socrates' treatment of Theaetetus' third definition, and possibly to recall the debate on knowledge and belief in the *Meno*, where belief was transformed into knowledge not merely by adding an account, but by uncovering the grounds of its being true, something it would not be perverse to describe as its *logos*.

13

The later dialectic:
the *Sophist* and the *Statesman*

The sophists had developed the technique of cross-examination to a fine art: their word-battles made use of systematic questioning as a weapon to refute an opponent's thesis. Socrates made use of the sophistical questioning technique to test definitions for consistency; he insisted on applying it to seriously held positions in order to explore their interior logic, not merely to intellectual aunt sallies to demonstrate his intellectual combat skills. As Plato struggled to understand the nature of knowledge, and to formulate an adequate epistemology, he saw that the dialectical method could have a use beyond mere consistency-testing. Once the questioning has been used to refute false opinions and to reduce someone to a state of bewildered ignorance, it can be used again to uncover truths. In the state of bewildered ignorance questioning is still possible, but questioning implies the possession of at least sufficient knowledge to formulate the question. The application of further questioning to a mind made ignorant and bewildered by questioning leads to recollection. This is the theory presented in the *Meno*.

In the *Republic* dialectic is developed a stage further: the application of the questioning technique to the hypothetical conclusions of the sciences leads to the ultimate form of knowledge, the knowledge of the Good and of the other Forms as they stand in relation to the Good. The process of reasoning from the Good to its relation to the other Forms is a positive, deductive, dialectical process.

In the *Phaedrus* Socrates is made to present an account of dialectic which introduces a quite new idea of what it is. It is a skill in collecting together and in division. It is the skill of seeing as a unity the scattered multiplicity that belongs under one Idea and of bringing it under a common definition, and the skill of separating out the various subclasses which belong under a single Idea, dividing them not arbitrarily or whimsically, but according to their natural relations with each other. The method of bringing together and separating out is illustrated at length in the *Sophist* and the *Statesman*. It was important enough in the philosophical and scientific practice of the members of Plato's Academy to be satirized.

The method clearly has some relation to the notion of dialectic presented in the *Republic*. The method of bringing together is analogous to the quest for the ultimate principles of things. The method of separating out is analogous to the reasoning from the Idea of the Good to the Forms to which it gives intelligibility. There is some degree of resemblance, but also a marked difference. The dialectic of the *Republic* is concerned with the forms of reasoning required in order to attain intuition of the ultimate first principle, and to discover what relation that principle has to the intelligible realities that depend on it. The dialectic of the *Phaedrus* is concerned with investigating the complex patterns of relationships that exist amongst classes, their inclusion in one another, their membership of one another. Dialectic in the dialogues up to the *Republic* seems formally to be one thing, a technique of systematic questioning, but applied to different object-matter with different functions and different results. The dialectic of the later dialogues is not a technique of questioning; it is a process of systematic classification. Its development represents a move to a more clearly logical and a more realistic view of dialectic. The dialectic presented in the *Republic* is heavily influenced by the metaphysics of the Theory of Forms, and above all by the position of the Idea of Good as the ultimate principle of intelligibility in the universe. The account given of dialectic is embedded in an account of the intellectual and moral development of the ideal philosopher ruler; it emphasizes those aspects of the dialectic that are crucially important to someone who strives to attain the most perfect and complete insight into the foundations of value. The later dialectic owes more to the classificatory procedures of rigorous and methodical scientific thinkers and less to the contemplative intellectual ascent of a speculative philosopher. Plato seems, in these later discussions of dialectic, to be responding to a major problem that is left by the account of dialectic given in the *Republic*, namely, that scientific knowledge seems to remain devoid of any satisfactory epistemological grounding until the intuition of the Idea of the Good is attained; but once the Idea of the Good is attained, the person who knows and understands it seems capable, in principle, of an infallible omniscience in the field of the intelligible. Understanding the principle of all intelligibility once he sees any other intelligible Form in the radiance of the Good, he should be able to know, understand, and give an account of it. The account and exemplification of dialectic in the later dialogues, on the other hand, presents it as a technique that can be applied to class concepts, to ideas of kinds, without any need for an ascent to a hypothetical supreme cognitive experience of the absolute ground of being, intelligibility, and value.

The structure of the method of separating out is of particular interest: it proceeds by the continual division of a class until a satisfactory definition is attained. The most famous example is the somewhat frivolous definition of the angler in the *Sophist*. The separating-out is done as follows.

We start the definition with the very general notion of an expert, a *technikos*, a man who possesses a *techne*, an art or skill. The notion of *techne* is then disarticulated by continual division until we come to the angler. Interestingly, the examples Plato himself gives show a careful and quite conscious avoidance of bisection of a class by using a term and its negation; in the derivation of the angler, for example, acquisition by force is divided into 'by hunting' and 'by fighting', not 'by hunting' and 'not by hunting'. The discussion of dialectic in the *Statesman* makes it clear that this reflects a serious philosophical concern of Plato's to avoid defining into existence Forms or classes which would correspond to no more than *ad hoc* divisions of classes.

The elaborate tree shown on p. 142 demonstrates one way of systematically disarticulating the class of Experts (there are evidently many others) so as to uncover the definition of the angler: an expert in the art of acquisition by force who hunts fish, living things inhabiting water, and hooks them by day. The example is cumbersome and comical: the method is thoroughly sensible.

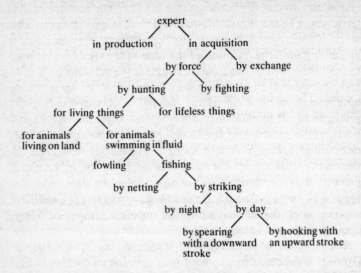

The dialectical processes of bringing together and separating out derive their validity from the relations which exist amongst the Ideas. It is clear even in the imperfectly thought-out version of the Theory of Forms presented in the *Republic* that the Ideas are not absolutely separate realities: all other Ideas stand in a relation of dependence to the Idea of the Good, the Intelligible Realm has a structure. Plato acknowledges quite explicitly in the *Sophist* that the Ideas have complex relationships with each other, that there is a weaving together of Ideas which is the basis of all our reasoning.

In principle, the dialectic of bringing together and separating out seems to be concerned with relations amongst the Ideas: in practice the Eleatic Stranger, who leads the discussions in the *Sophist* and the *Statesman*, seems to be concerned with relations amongst classes of things, usually of human beings. Provided that there exists an Idea corresponding to every class, then the analysis of relations amongst classes of things and the analysis of the relation amongst the Ideas will be equivalent activities.

A large section of the *Sophist* is occupied by the Eleatic

Stranger's presentation of a series of dialectical exercises designed to uncover the nature of the sophist. This accords with his declared intention early in the dialogue to offer an account of the sophist, the statesman, and the philosopher. The sequence of sophist-hunts is amusing in a somewhat heavy-footed way, and allows Plato to give full expression to his contempt for the species. The technique used in each case is identical with that exhibited in the definition of the angler. We are not to take the various analyses too seriously; what Plato is doing is more malicious satire than philosophical analysis. After constructing six characterizations of the sophist by application of the method of separation, the Stranger pauses for breath:

STRANGER. First let us stand still and catch our breath, and while we're resting let us take count of the number of guises in which the sophist has appeared to us. I think the first was as a paid hunter of rich young men.

THEAETETUS. Yes.

STRANGER. And the second, as some kind of trader in soul-improvement.

THEAETETUS. Indeed.

STRANGER. Third he appeared as a retailer of such items?

THEAETETUS. Yes, and fourthly as a learning-wright dealing in products of his own creation.

STRANGER. Your memory's correct. I'll have a go at recalling the fifth case myself: he was some kind of athlete in verbal combat specialising in eristic.

THEAETETUS. Right.

STRANGER. The sixth was a bit dubious, but we still agreed to consider him a purger of minds who gets rid of opinions that get in the way of learning.

THEAETETUS. Exactly.

STRANGER. But don't you see that when someone derives his name from a single art, but appears to possess many kinds of knowledge, there has to be something wrong with this impression: it is evident that anyone who is under such an impression with regard to any particular art is quite unable to perceive the focal point of the person's various accomplishments and accordingly characterizes their possessor by a plurality of names instead of a single one. (231 d–232 a)

The Stranger's remark points to an important issue; it may be possible to cut up a particular class in many different ways, equally, it may be possible to produce a variety of different characterizations of the class named by a particular term; Plato is warning us that there is no guarantee that, just because we have achieved a coherent and consistent analysis by using the method of collection and separation, we have uncovered the nature of the class in question. The formal coherence and consistency of a given application of the dialectic of gathering and separation guarantees no more than that the characterization derived from it will also be consistent and coherent; there is no guarantee it will also be a correct characterization identifying the essential nature of the particular class.

The *Sophist* and its companion-piece the *Statesman* are presented by Plato as continuing the conversation begun in the *Theaetetus*. Stylistic differences make it clear that the *Sophist* and the *Statesman* were written rather after the *Theaetetus*. The literary device of connecting the conversations together may be merely a way of creating a sense of unity and connectedness amongst Plato's works, or may invite the reader of the *Sophist* to read the *Theaetetus* as a preface. If Plato is suggesting a significant connection between dialogues, it may be that the *Sophist* contains an implicit answer to the question discussed in the *Theaetetus*: the *Theaetetus* asks what knowledge is, the *Sophist* exhibits the nature of knowledge and the dialectical methods by which it is attained. Given the importance of definitions in Plato's philosophical thinking, such a connection between the dialogues is not impossible. The early dialogues show Socrates searching for definitions and testing them; in the *Republic* Socrates claims that the true dialectician will be able to define the Good and to defend his definition against all attempted refutations: here in the *Sophist* the Eleatic Stranger gives a lengthy and impressive exhibition of how to construct definitions by the method of collection and division, and argues for the existence of patterns of relations amongst the Forms, which explain how it is that such definitional strategies work. The rigorous application of the dialectical method of classification will enable the attainment of scientific knowledge that is based on an ordered account of what is under discussion, laying out its elements in their natural relation to each other: the elements are not, as in one of the arguments in the *Theaetetus*, unintelligible, but are themselves classes to each of which corresponds an intelligible Idea. The application, however, must be rigorous and carefully tested; this dialectical method does not carry the promise of infallibility that attends the dialectical descent from the vision of the Idea of Good in the *Republic*.

A specific development of the Theory of Forms takes place in the *Sophist*, which represents the fruit of Plato's application of his dialectical analysis to the relations existing among the 'greatest kinds'. The Ideas picked out by the Eleatic Stranger as determining some of the greatest kinds are those of Being, Motion, Rest, Sameness, and Difference. A complex dialectical analysis uncovers the relations which hold amongst these greatest kinds.

(*a*) All five kinds participate in Being, Sameness, and Difference.

(*b*) Motion does not share in Rest, nor Rest in Motion.

(*c*) The Idea of Difference is the Idea of Non-Being.

All five kinds exist and therefore participate in Being; each kind is identical with itself and all kinds therefore participate in Sameness; each kind is distinct from every other kind, and so each participates in Difference. If we descend to the level of classes less general than the greatest kinds, the same must also hold of them. Whatever Xs may be, the class of Xs is identical with itself, and its members are sufficiently similar to each other in virtue of their common X-ness for us to be certain the class of Xs participates in Sameness; the class of Xs is distinct from all other classes by being the class of Xs, and its members both differ from each other sufficiently to be identified as distinct individuals, and differ from all non-Xs precisely in that they are Xs and the non-Xs are not, so it follows that they must participate in Difference too. Everything that exists, and every class of existent things participates in Being. Every class, then, participates in Being, Sameness, and Difference.

Motion and Rest cannot participate in or be predicated of each other: they are mutually exclusive. It is not only the case that they do not participate in each other; logically, they cannot do so.

Predicating motion of rest, or rest of motion, would produce precisely the sort of contradiction Plato diagnosed in the *Phaedo* as arising if one predicates death of the soul if the soul is thought of as life and the principle of life.

At first sight the identification of Non-Being with Difference may seem bizarre and gratuitous. The Eleatic Stranger makes it clear (259) that he is not holding the absurd view that non-existence is identical with Difference: 'Let no-one say of us that we explain Non-Being as the opposite of Being and dare to assert that it exists! For we long since said farewell to talk of any opposite of it, whether it exists or not, whether it is definable or utterly indefinable.' The Non-Being the Eleatic Stranger is discussing is the general concept corresponding to the use of 'not' in such expressions as 'not large', 'not just', and so forth. It is not the Form of Non-Existence; there can be no such thing. It is the Form of Not-Being-of-such-and-such-a-kind, the Form of Other-than—. The identification of this Form with the Form of Difference is uncontroversial.

There is, however, an aspect of Plato's identification of the Form of Non-Being with the Form of Difference that is much less uncontroversial, and which represents a philosophical insight of quite startling originality. Plato not only asserts that the Form of Non-Being is the Form of Difference, he also asserts equally clearly that there is no Form of Non-Existence apart from this. This denial implies the acceptance of an analysis of negative existential statements, statements, that is to say, of the form 'There is no X', or 'Zs do not exist', or 'the Y does not exist', which entails that all such statements can be expressed without loss of meaning in terms of positive existential statements, statements of sameness and statements of difference. There is, Plato is saying, no class of non-entities. He is not, of course, denying that there is a class of non-referential names, names which do not refer to anything; what he does, and surely rightly, deny, is that there are individual non-entities and classes of non-entities to which those names refer.

The Stranger argues that all discourse depends on the weaving together of the Forms (259 e). If all classes were utterly separate from each other, discourse would collapse totally. Discourse works because of the relations holding amongst the Forms; if the Forms were not interwoven with each other, then the world would consist of utterly separate classes and there would be nothing to be said. Just as a Heraclitan world of pure flux gives language no basis unless there are fixed intelligible patterns underlying and manifested in the flux, so a world of completely separate, unrelated classes, gives no basis for knowledge or understanding.

In order to make statements in language, our utterance must have a certain complexity. A name or noun by itself asserts nothing: it has a meaning, but no assertoric power. Equally, a verb or predicate by itself asserts nothing: a statement is made only when a name and a verb are combined together.

> 'Theaetetus' states nothing.
> 'Flies' states nothing.
> 'Theaetetus flies' is a statement capable of being true or false.

The point Plato is making is logical, not grammatical. It might be the case that a complex assertion (in answer to a question, for example) could be made by uttering or writing a single word. Such an example would not dent Plato's claim: in any such case an analysis of the context would show that the conventions of language-use give a logically discernible complexity to the expression in question.

The *Statesman* is the immediate sequel to the *Sophist*. In both dialogues the Eleatic Stranger leads discussions, which are presented as stages in an attempt to define the sophist, the statesman, and the philosopher. There is, despite the initial promise of one, no direct discussion of the philosopher: Plato may well have decided there was no need to offer a specific definition of him, given the implications of the definitions he offers of the sophist and the statesman. He has shown the nature of the philosopher in the discussion of the statesman, and shown the true nature of the philosopher's fake image, his living parody, in the discussion of the sophist.

The definitional technique of the *Statesman*, like that of the *Sophist*, is based on the dialectical process of separating-out. The enthusiasm of the Young Socrates, who is the Stranger's interlocutor in the *Statesman*, leads him to an over-hasty division of the art of herding into herding men and herding beasts. The Stranger warns him that, if he is going to divide off a part of a species, he should ensure that the part he separates off is itself a species. Not every part of a species is necessarily a species. Exactly what this tells us about the structure of the realm of Forms is not clear, but it indicates at least that it is not possible to define a new Form into existence by a whimsical verbal distinction. There is a Form corresponding to every class, but not every linguistic expression which has the same grammatical status as a class-name is for the Stranger necessarily a class-name. There is, then, no guarantee that there is a Form corresponding to everything that looks like the name of a class. The Stranger gives an illuminating example: the Greeks have the bad habit of dividing the human race in two: Greeks and barbarians. But the barbarians differ in race and nationality: the barbarians do not constitute a species. The barbarians are not a species of the genus Man, though they are part of that genus; there is no Idea of Barbarian.

Plato spends little time expounding the distinction he is making; it is none the less an important distinction. Plato is refusing to succumb to the bewitchment of language. He accepts in the *Parmenides* that there is a Form corresponding to every class; he refuses to infer from this that there is a Form corresponding to every shared name. He does not deny that the term 'barbarian' has meaning and reference, he denies only that it names a species. There exist, then, collectivities which are not species: some of these collectivities are parts of species, some, we may infer, are parts of a number of species, but they do not form new species. This distinction should warn us to be on our guard againt any temptation to assume too readily that Plato is talking in the later dialogues only about logical and linguistic problems; his metaphysical interests may be much less to the fore than in the *Republic*, but they have not been laid aside. Whatever the Theory of Forms is by the time Plato is writing the *Sophist* and the *Statesman*, it is still not reduced to a theory of the meaning and reference of general terms.

The world of Forms is prior to the world of things: the classes that exist in the world of things represent the Forms, the relations amongst the classes represent relations amongst the Forms. This relation between the world of sense-experience and the world of Intelligible Reality is for the Plato of the later dialogues the ground of all discourse and all understanding. The structure of the world of the Forms is reflected in the permanent patterns which are the essential structure of the world of things. There are also shifting, transient patterns in the world of things that are not images of anything in the world of Forms: human beings may take an interest in such transient patterns and give them names, but such names will not then pick out genuine species or be evidence for the existence of Forms.

14

The living world and the God
who made it

The Forms are eternal and changeless. The world of our everyday experience is an image of the world of Forms. We cannot understand anything in the visible world until we see it in relation to the stable patterns which exist in the intelligible realm. The world of everyday life is an image in time of the intelligible order which exists in eternity; a flowing, changing image.

The earlier dialogues contain few indications as to how the visible world came into existence. Are we to imagine the perfect world of Forms spontaneously begetting an imperfect, mutable image of itself? There is something absurd in the notion. Even if we accept Plato's arguments that the visible world requires the existence of the Forms if knowledge and understanding are to be possible, there seems no obvious reason why the intelligible world would ever need the visible world to exist.

There are suggestions even in the *Republic* that Plato accepted the idea of a Divine Demiurge, a Creator-God who is responsible for the existence of the world of things; not, of course, a God who creates the world from nothing as does the God of classical Christian theism, but a God who creates as the artist or craftsman creates. Socrates speaks of 'the maker of the senses' (507 c) and 'the maker of the heavens' (530 a). Confusingly, he also speaks of the God making the Form of the Bed (597 b–c). If we infer from Socrates' talk of a 'maker of the heavens' that Plato is telling us the visible world owes its existence to the work of a Divine Creator, then the reference to the God making the Form of the Bed would seem to imply that the Divine Creator also produced the Forms. There is nothing in the rest of the dialogues to support the inference that Plato believed the Forms themselves were created by God, on the contrary, their eternal existence is constantly emphasized: lower Forms depend on their participation on higher Forms for their nature and existence; that eternal pattern of dependence is something quite distinct from coming to be as the result of a divine act of creation. The absence of any systematic discussion in the *Republic* of the origin of the world of things suggests that Socrates' casual references to the Craftsman God may be no more than that, the use of familiar images to make a point in discussion, but without any doctrinal emphasis. There is no clear indication that when writing the *Republic* Plato had any coherent theory of creation. None the less, the suggestion is there, and the problem of the origin of the world of material, sensible things remains to be solved.

The *Statesman*, the *Philebus*, and the *Timaeus* contain Plato's solution to the problem of the world's origin. The *Statesman* contains a lengthy mythical account of the divine government of the world. The cyclic motion of the heavens is due to the God's periodic action, infusing new vitality into them; as the power he gives them wanes, the movement of the heavens reverses until he once again revitalizes them. When all things are moving under his control, the God governs and supervises the pattern of the world's revolution, establishing lesser deities and spirits in positions of responsibility over the various kinds of living thing. As the God's influence wanes, the inferior spirits withdraw their influence too, and an immense upheaval occurs. The myth with its strong echoes of Empedoclean speculative cosmology, is located in a discussion of the nature of kingship and statesmanship: it is not a literal account of how the God relates to the material world. The myth's emphasis on the world's need for the God's vitalizing influence is significant: the world is more than mere matter.

The *Philebus* contains an important passage which spells out more explicitly what is only hinted at in the mythical tale in the *Statesman*. The *Philebus* is mainly concerned with the nature of the good life: Socrates argues that neither pleasure alone nor intellect alone is sufficient for the good life; what is required is a mixture of the two. He points to the significant contrast between Limit and the Unlimited, a familiar commonplace of Pythagorean philosophical speculation, and identifies the mixed life as belonging to the third class which arises from the determination of the Unlimited by Limit. He now moves to explain more clearly what this unfamiliar distinction means, and to relate it to the distinction between body and soul.

Our bodies are composed of the four elements earth, water, air, and fire: the elements that exist in our bodies depend on the elements which compose the material universe as a whole. Just as certain amounts of each of the four elements combine together to constitute our bodies, so the totality of the four elements constitutes the body of the Universe.

SOCRATES. We would surely say our body has a soul?

PROTARCHUS. Clearly.

SOCRATES. Where from, my dear Protarchus?—unless the body of Universe is itself besouled—for it has the same constituents as ours apart from their general superiority.

PROTARCHUS. Evidently, Socrates, there is nowhere else it could come from.

SOCRATES. Indeed, Protarchus, we could scarcely think that when of the four things, Limit, the Unlimited, the Combination of both, and the Cause, it is this fourth which exists within everything, which provides us with a soul, instilling physical fitness, the healing of physical frailties, in general producing harmony and health and being regarded as universal wisdom; and when all those same (four) things exist throughout the heavens and the major divisions of the heavens in a fine and pure state—that it should not be the contriver of the nature of the fairest and worthiest of things!

PROTARCHUS. That would indeed be an absurdity.

SOCRATES. Well, let us avoid such error and for preference argue the view we have so often expounded: the Universe contains Limit aplenty, an equal measure of Unlimit, and also a potent Cause which brings order and arrangement to years, seasons, and months—it well deserves the names 'Wisdom' and 'Mind'.

PROTARCHUS. It does indeed.

SOCRATES. And presumably wisdom and mind could never occur apart from the soul?

PROTARCHUS. Of course not.

SOCRATES. And would you not say it is by the power of the Cause that the nature of Zeus acquired its kingly soul and its kingly mind, and that the other deities acquired those fine qualities they like to be named after?

PROTARCHUS. Indeed.

SOCRATES. What we are saying is of some considerable significance, Protarchus: it is in full accord with the declaration of those who long ago proclaimed that Mind is ever the ruler of all. (30 a–d)

This whole Universe, Plato is asserting, is a living entity: like us it has both body and soul. The Cosmic Soul possesses a mind: in virtue of its intelligence and wisdom the Cosmic Soul rules, governs, and orders the entire Universe. The powers we recognize as gods, even Zeus himself, owe their lives, their wisdom, their understanding, all their noble qualities to the Cosmic Soul.

The Universe of which we are all part is a vast living organism: it is a living and intelligent reality. Its order and structure derive from the actions and decisions of the Cosmic Mind. The Universe determines its own pattern of organization; it does so by an intelligent imposition of Limit upon the Unlimited.

Exactly what Plato means by 'Limit' and 'Unlimited' is not immediately clear. The terms are familiar from Pythagorean lists of opposites, and the Pythagorean reference is certainly deliberate. He intends at the least to imply that the rational order the Cosmic Mind creates is rooted in mathematical relations.

How the Unlimited is determined by Limit is made a little clearer in the account of Creation contained in the *Timaeus*. In this dialogue the Demiurge creates the universe as a living being modelled on the Intelligible Living Being—that pattern of Ideas which is the eternal prototype of the created Universe. The Demiurge creates the Cosmic Soul by mingling together Being, Sameness, and Difference. The Body of the Universe is created from the four elements earth, water, air, and fire. The four elements derive, according to the somewhat obscure account Plato offers in the *Timaeus*, from the shaping or forming of an original 'receptacle'; as it takes on the characteristics of one or other of the regular solids, it becomes one or other of the four elements.

The Demiurge creates the universe using the eternal Forms as model. This act of creation is also the imposition of Limit on the Unlimited. The receptacle, space, is an aspect of the Unlimited: the shaping and forming of the receptacle on the model of the regular geometrical solids is also the imposition of Limit on the Unlimited.

The Demiurge of the *Timaeus* is a fascinating and puzzling figure. The Demiurge is coeternal with the Forms, but is neither an individual Form nor the totality of the Forms. We may be tempted to identify the Demiurge with the Cosmic Soul, until we realize the Demiurge created the Cosmic Soul.

It is possible to read the creation story of the *Timaeus* as a metaphor of the operation of the human intellect, to interpret the account of creation as a semi-allegorical account of the intellectual construction of an intelligible world and of the creation of order in the world of perceptible reality. Tempting and economical as such as interpretation is, it has no real textual support. It is also unnecessary: the creation story fills an important gap in Plato's philosophical theorizing: now, for the first time, we have an account of the origin of the visible world which offers at least some rationale for its existence. Without the creation story the world of Forms possesses a necessity of some kind, but the visible world is gratuitous. The *Timaeus* offers an explanation. The Forms are not the only eternal existents: a vastly powerful creative mind (the Demiurge) and a 'receptacle' (space) are also eternal. The Demiurge creates the Universe in his own image: it is a lesser, created god possessing life and intelligence which echo the attributes of the Creator-God. Whether this account should be interpreted as referring literally to a process of coming to be, or whether it is a metaphor intended to disclose the structure of the Universe as it is and always has been must remain a matter of conjecture.

Plato's dialogues contain exactly as much of his philosophical thought as he judged appropriate to make public from time to time. Plato was not only a writer and a thinker, he was also a teacher. Aristotle's works contain evidence of developments of the Theory of Ideas which are not present in any of Plato's published works. For the last nineteen years of Plato's life, Aristotle was a member of the Academy; he was in a position to know what Plato taught his students and what he discussed with them. In the absence of convincing evidence to the contrary his account of Plato's thought may be accepted as accurate.

Aristotle tells us of three major developments to the Theory of Ideas:

(a) Plato derived the Forms from two more fundamental principles, the One and the Indefinite Dyad.
(b) Plato taught that the Forms are numbers.
(c) Plato taught that there is a class of mathematical entities intermediate between the Forms and visible things.

The Theory of Ideas as it was discussed in the Academy during the latter years of Plato's life seems to have had a stronger mathematical colouring than anything presented in the published writings.

Exactly how we are to interpret the doctrinal developments Aristotle records is not at all clear. The mathematical entities present the least problems; they are eternal individual entities, not the Idea of Triangularity or the Form of the Circle, but a vast multiplicity of individual triangles and circles which geometry can prove to exist. Indeed Plato may well have thought mathematics provided proofs of the existence of the mathematical entities; the language mathematicians use frequently suggests he was not alone in that belief. The mathematical entities are eternal and immaterial like the Forms: unlike the Forms they are individual entities, not universal Ideas.

The Forms are numbers, but they are not identified with the mathematical numbers. What exactly Plato may have meant by this claim is not easy to determine with certainty. Whatever the precise significance of the identification of the Forms with numbers, it is beyond doubt rooted in Pythagorean number metaphysics. It may be that Plato thought of the Forms not so much as individual numbers but rather as ratios or formulae, in which case he might have thought of a Form-number as the formula of the intelligible structure of the essence of a class. For Plato, mathematics was about the relationships amongst numbers and quantities abstractly considered as they are studied in arithmetic, the properties of points, lines, surfaces, and solids as they are studied by geometry, but also the relations of musical sounds and the spatial patterns and the properties of the motion of the heavenly bodies as they are studied by astronomy. Given the suggestion of the *Timaeus* that the four elements are expressions of the four regular solids, we already see a mathematical structure to all shapes, all quantities, to all sounds and sequences of sounds, to the structure of the heavens, the patterns of movement of the heavenly bodies and the relations amongst them, and the nature and organization of the elements; it seems no small step to accepting that the structure of all classes expresses something fundamentally mathematical.

Computers have familiarized us with the idea that concepts and structures which seem at first sight remote from mathematics can be mapped on to a binary digital system: had Plato been alive today, he would have found the computer a suggestive example of how things can be represented in a purely mathematical language based on the most restricted range of fundamental values.

The derivation of the Ideas from the One and the Indefinite Dyad is more difficult to understand. There are indications in the dialogues that Plato was trying to uncover the ultimate principles which account for the structure of the intelligible world and of the visible Universe: in the *Sophist* we are introduced to the five Greatest Kinds, Being, Sameness, Difference, Motion, and Rest, and in the *Philebus* we meet the two principles Limit and the Unlimited, whose mixture is brought about by Mind. Once Plato accepts the importance of the interweaving of Forms, and their complex hierarchical ordering, it is natural to conclude he inquired determinedly into the ultimate basis of the common features shared by the Forms, and found the Pythagorean list of opposites an inspiring guide to a level of analysis deeper than that represented in the arguments of the *Sophist* and the *Philebus*.

In the *Philebus* Plato presents another aspect of this deeper analysis when he argues that the Good must be analysed into 'Beauty, symmetry, and Truth' (65 a). This analysis may well be led by psychological considerations: in the *Philebus* Plato is discussing the importance of pleasure in human life and develops a more complex and penetrating understanding of human psychology than is represented in any earlier dialogue. In the *Philebus* Plato accepts the importance of pleasure as a significant element in the good life; he abandons finally the pure, austere, but potentially arid intellectualism of the *Phaedo*. This change in Plato's psychology is part and parcel of a whole pattern of transformation consequent on his enhanced awareness of the importance of dynamic aspects of the structure of the Universe.

Eventually Plato integrated his theory of the nature of the Good with his theory of Ideal numbers; he astounded an audience that came to hear him lecture on 'The Good' by starting with geometrical considerations and ending with the assertion that 'Limit is the one good' (or perhaps, 'that good is ultimately one'; the phrase presents problems of translation).

15

Plato's last words: The *Laws*

In old age Plato remained intellectually active. His later dialogues show a mind still flexible and still fertile. No doubt his contact with younger thinkers in the Academy helped him retain his own intellectual vitality. The later dialogues may lack the sparkling humour and the vivid portraiture which make the earlier dialogues so readable, but they present new ideas, new forms of argument, and new techniques of dialectical reasoning; they address new questions, and approach familiar questions in new ways.

The *Laws* is Plato's last work. It is a substantial work, as long as the *Republic*. It suffers from flaws of style and a certain dryness: it is the work of an old man determined to write down and publish ideas he believes important. Plato is racing the calendar as he writes the *Laws*; style is of little concern to him. And what he has to say is new.

It is clear from the *Republic* that Plato's political ideal was that the state should be governed by philosophers who would know with certainty the moral principles which should inform the social order. Sadly the one serious opportunity he had to turn a ruler into a philosopher failed utterly. The ideal remained, and Plato's Academy continued to furnish the sort of education a philosopher-ruler would need, but Plato came to accept that the philosopher-ruler might prove an unattainable ideal.

In the *Statesman* the Eleatic Stranger uses the techniques of definition by continual separating out to demonstrate that the art of government is indeed a form of knowledge. A ruler who possesses that knowledge will be able to decide political questions with wisdom and understanding. Failing such a ruler, the state should be governed by law.

Law, unfortunately, cannot produce justice and goodness in every possible circumstance: it is not possible to formulate the law so as to take account of every possible variation in human conduct. Law has, of necessity, a schematic character.

If we cannot expect to have the state governed by a succession of philosopher-rulers, who possess the knowledge and wisdom to establish order and justice and to rule the community to the benefit of all, then the best we can hope for is a statesman-lawgiver who can furnish the state with a wisely constructed system of laws.

There is a science of statecraft. The true statesman possesses a body of knowledge which enables him to make wise and rational political and legal decisions.

Plato now argues that it is the presence and absence of statecraft in the rulers of a society which determines its political merit even more than the specific kind of constitution it possesses. Monarchy is of itself neither good nor bad: a statesman-king is the best of rulers, an ignorant tyrant the worst. Government by the few may be by an enlightened aristocracy or a benighted wealth-drunk oligarchy. A democracy may be guided by reason and knowledge, in which case it would be a form of good government, albeit the weakest form of good government: a democracy lacking statecraft will be a form of bad government, though, given the inefficiency and vacillation characteristic of democratic decision-making, it will be less evil than an efficient tyranny would be.

This theoretical shift now allows Plato to take a much more flexible view of the constitutional arrangements possible in a just and morally educative society. The essential requirements are that the constitution and the laws be founded on sound knowledge and rational judgement, and that changes to them be determined only by those who possess adequate knowledge of the science of statecraft.

As Plato advanced into old age, philosopher-rulers remained in depressingly short supply. On occasion states might seek philosophical advice on legal and constitutional matters: they showed little sign of handing over supreme power to Plato and his colleagues. Even had the citizens of Athens decided to hand over supreme political power to Plato, he would have found it difficult to institute anything like the society of the *Republic*: the citizens showed no signs of possessing the moral qualities required for life in an Ideal State.

In the *Laws* Plato sets himself a new problem: he sets out to design the constitution and laws for a new colony. Plato's constitutional and legal proposals are intended to be taken seriously. The Ideal State of the *Republic* is an image of political perfection we shall never see realized in full: the state whose design is presented in the *Laws* could be brought into being by any suitable group of colonists who possess the political will.

Plato names his imaginary colony 'Magnesia'. It is to have a limited citizenship: there will be 5,040 landowning citizens. Each will receive an inalienable allotment of land and will be allowed to possess private property up to four times the value of the original allocation. The land allotments are to be farmed and every citizen is to provide for his own household. Aliens can obtain permission to reside in Magnesia, but only if they have skills which are of use to Magnesia. The residence of aliens is normally limited to twenty years. To the embarrassment of the modern reader, Plato accepts the institution of slavery in the new state.

The new colony will be sited about eighty *stadia* (ten miles) inland, and the state will maintain harbours of high quality on the coast. The land will be of sufficient quality and extent to grow the food the population needs.

The citizens will be divided into four classes on the basis of property. The inalienable land allotments are to be allocated by lot. The whole state is divided into twelve segments and the location of the lot which falls to a citizen will determine to which of twelve artificial tribes he belongs. The allotments will be as equal as possible: profitable effort will enable a citizen to increase his wealth and rise in class. Offices will be allocated to the members of the different classes in a way that reflects their different status: unequals will be treated unequally, as Plato's conception of social justice requires. Plato designs a complicated set of arrangements for the election of state officials, both civil and military. He provides Magnesia with an Assembly of the whole body of adult male citizens, and a Council of 360 members. A subcommittee of one twelfth of the Council will exercise executive powers for a month at a time. Each of the four property classes will provide ninety Councillors: 180 members will be elected from each class, and the ninety Councillors chosen by lottery from amongst those elected. All citizens who serve or have served in the army have the right to vote for the thirty-seven Guardians of the Law, the chief legal officers of the state. A system of law courts exists at local, tribal, and state level.

The body of citizens will elect a board of Inquisitors whose right and duty it is to examine the conduct of all the officers of the state. Plato lays great emphasis on the importance of the Inquisitors: they will maintain the stability and moral health of the state. He recognizes, however, that even an Inquisitor may be brought to trial. (Frivolous accusations against high officers of state are unlikely since an unsuccessful prosecutor will find himself subject to severe penalties.)

Above all the other institutions of Magnesia's complex legal and administrative system stands the Nocturnal Council. This Council is composed of the most senior Guardians of the Law and other citizens of high distinction each of whom chooses a younger man of at least thirty who, subject to the approval of his fellow councillors, is given a seat. The Nocturnal Council meets before dawn to engage in the study of philosophy so that the Councillors attain the fullest possible understanding of the rational principles which underlie and justify the laws of Magnesia, to study reports of the legal systems of other states so as to make improvements and amendments to the legal system of Magnesia, and to ensure the state's officers teach the truth as they carry out their duties.

Magnesia has a state religion with a formal cult and an official priesthood. All citizens are required to avoid three pernicious heresies:

(*a*) that there are no gods,
(*b*) that there are gods, but they take no care of mankind,
(*c*) that the gods are easy to appease and persuade by prayers and
        sacrifices.

Heresy is punished by the law: every attempt is made to persuade the heretic of his error; if he persists he may be imprisoned, if he remains incorrigible he will be put to death. This provision of the Magnesian legal code may shock a modern reader: Plato saw the three heresies as undermining morality and consequently as a serious attack on the state's stability.

The stability of the state requires that the citizens respect and obey the law. Plato demands that the citizens obey the law, but the obedience he demands is that voluntary obedience appropriate to human beings. The law should be obeyed because it is good, not simply because it is the law. Each law is to be accompanied by an explanatory preamble which sets out the rationale for the law. The law forms and shapes conduct; it imposes and at the same time teaches right conduct.

Plato gives a detailed account of an astounding range of legal provisions: he specifies both the laws to be enacted and the penalties to be imposed on transgressors. The detail he provides is evidence of how seriously he takes his work of constitutional and legal design in the *Laws*.

Education was an important theme in the *Republic*: it is an important theme in the *Laws*. The Minister of Education holds, Plato says, the greatest of all the state's great offices. The education of the young is of crucial importance to the moral well-being of the state. Their education must be based on a sound understanding of human psychology. The infant's experience of things begins with sensations of pleasure and pain: if children are to become virtuous, then their feelings must be channelled in appropriate directions. Children must learn to feel pleasure and pain, to love and hate appropriately: when they grow up they will come to understand the reasons underlying the training they have received. A sound system of education requires the integration of intellect and emotion.

Education is a formative process involving the total person. Education begins in the womb: Plato requires pregnant women to take plenty of exercise to ensure the healthy development of the baby. Once the child is born, swaddling clothes are to be used to keep its body in good shape. For three years the child's nurses will carry it about with them, ensuring it is stimulated by frequent movement until it is capable of walking itself without putting undue strain on its limbs. The young child is to be treated considerately and carefully, neither indulged nor maltreated. Life should be made pleasant for the young child, but not to the extent that the child becomes a pleasure-glutton.

From 4 to 7 the child is taught through play. The officials who supervise the children's play will encourage them to develop the maximum degree of skill and versatility in the use of both hands and both feet. If possible all children should grow up ambidextrous.

From 6 onwards boys and girls will be separated. The boys will start to learn the martial arts: the girls may follow the lessons too if they have the inclination. The children will learn to dance and to wrestle, the boys will also learn the use of weapons and the skills of armed combat.

The games the children play, the dances they learn, will be fixed by being made sacred: they must not be allowed to change randomly. Changing the games children play has an effect on their character-development; once the right games have been determined no casual change is to be permitted. Games and dances will become part of religion.

The general curriculum Plato proposes for Magnesia is derived directly from the curriculum proposed in the *Republic* for the education of the Guardians. In the *Republic* only the Ruling Class and their Auxiliaries need to be trained for military service: in Magnesia all citizens will be training for combat, since all citizens will be expected to defend the state if the need arises. In the *Republic* the Third Class of citizens has no real need of systematic education: they have no part to play in political decision-making and administration. In Magnesia the entire body of male citizens shares in important decisions, nominates and votes for officers of the state: all the citizens need an education similar to that of the Auxiliaries of the *Republic*, and this is precisely what Plato proposes. All the citizens of Magnesia will undergo a sound programme of physical training to prepare them for the demands of military service. Young men and women will both be trained in the use of weapons: if the whole army is needed in a war, the women might have to defend their own hearths and children. The programme of physical education will include a training in dance, including armoured dance. The general curriculum includes literature, music, and mathematics. Plato remains convinced of the need for stern censorship of the arts: he is opposed to citizens acting in tragedies and comedies, to frivolous versatility in musical performance. Uncontrolled poetical inspiration has no place in a rationally ordered society. Plato suggests that the *Laws* itself should provide a useful and exemplary textbook for literary study: he suggests the Minister of Education should ensure similarly valuable examples of verse and prose writing are sought out for pedagogical use, and that conversations, discussions, and speeches of the kind recorded in the *Laws* be committed to writing to become texts for study. Teachers will be expected to learn texts, to be able to declaim them effectively, and to put them to use in the educational programme.

The philosophical studies which form the apex of the higher education of the *Republic*'s Rulers are echoed in the philosophical studies of Magnesia's Nocturnal Council.

Family life is of great importance in Magnesia: the law imposes a duty of marriage on all citizens. A man is expected to marry between the ages of 25 and 30. Marriage partners should be chosen with an eye to the quality of offspring the couple might hope to produce, not as a financial investment. Excessive dowries, luxurious trousseaux, extravagant wedding celebrations are all criminal and invoke appropriate punishments. Adultery is a serious criminal offence. Extramarital sexual intercourse, whether heterosexual or homosexual, is to be discouraged and subjected to moral and social disapproval. If difficulties occur in a marriage, then the officers of the state will be responsible for attempting to bring about a reconciliation of husband and wife: if a reconciliation is impossible, then the couple should be divorced and seek new partners. If a marriage remains infertile after ten years, the couple are to divorce and seek new partners. Officers of the state will supervise the citizens' married lives to ensure they are lived in conformity with the spirit of the law.

Plato wishes to see common meals instituted in Magnesia: not only would he have men share a common table, as amongst Spartiates, women too should ideally share the common meals. This to us somewhat bizarre institution is designed to promote social cohesiveness and mitigate any tendencies to selfishness or greed which the possession of property might encourage. Indeed the citizens should be led to think of all their property as belonging ultimately to the state and themselves as beneficiary trustees rather than possessive owners.

The Guardians of the Law have the responsiblity for the care of orphans. The society should have the means and the resources to assist citizens who fall into need despite their own best efforts. In Magnesia no one will be reduced to abject poverty unless it is the person's own fault. Begging will never be justified: beggars will be expelled.

Despite the harshness of some of the laws Plato lays down, Magnesia will be a caring society. The law is designed to promote social stability and virtuous conduct; citizens who are victims of misfortune will easily find help. The duties of children to parents are emphasized, so are the society's duties to children.

Magnesia is a society very different from the Ideal State described in the *Republic*. In Magnesia the law is fixed and permanent unless the Nocturnal Council decides to change it. Change will in general be avoided. In matters other than those laid down by the law, the democratic vote of the citizen body, or the decisions of councillors or officers democratically nominated and elected will have great significance. The whole citizen body of Magnesia has the kind of education reserved to the Guardians in the *Republic*. The communism of wives and property established for the Guardians remains a theoretical ideal, but is in practice abandoned in the design of Magnesia. Plato seems to have realized the value of marriage and family life as a stabilizing element in the state. The constitution and laws of Magnesia owe not a little to the constitution and laws of Athens. They are evidently grounded in Plato's critical study of the political structures and institutions of Greek states. Magnesia is no mere replica of Athens; apart from the inclusion of elements drawn from foreign political systems, such as, for example, the inalienable allotments of land which existed in Sparta, Magnesia contains many elements which are either totally or partly the product of Plato's considerable capacity for creative political design.

In Magnesia the slaves and resident aliens perform many of the functions performed by the members of the Third Class in the *Republic*. Farming, however, which in the *Republic* would be one of the duties of the Third Class, is in Magnesia the duty of all the citizens, though the actual manual work may well be carried out by slaves. The citizens of Magnesia are to be politically responsible, well educated, soldier-farmers who, as a matter of civic duty, enforced if necessary by law, are directly involved in the selection of the state's officers. The most able and most virtuous citizens can attain supreme office as members of the Nocturnal Council. The class system has less significance in Magnesia than in the *Republic*: there are no obstacles to social mobility, and upward mobility is actively encouraged. In the *Republic* the Third Class receives little consideration: the whole social structure of the *Republic* expresses a profound pessimism about the moral and intellectual capacities of the majority of the citizenry who would make up this class. No such pessimism informs the design of Magnesia: the new colony is a moral enterprise, its laws and institutions ensure the citizens can be expected to conduct themselves virtuously and responsibly. Few will ever attain membership of the Nocturnal Council, but every citizen will have the opportunity to serve the state as councillor, priest, legal, civic, or military official. No such prospect attends the members of the *Republic*'s Third Class. Not even the Auxiliary Guardians of the *Republic* can expect to hold office as philosopher-rulers, whereas a citizen of Magnesia can, under the right circumstances, become a statesman-lawgiver as a member of the Nocturnal Council. Citizenship in Magnesia is a moral project: all tasks that might distract from the life of virtue are to be performed by slaves or resident aliens. The state is a school of morality.

When discussing the *Republic* I argued that the Basic *Polis*, the Frugal Community which Glaucon derides as a city fit only for pigs, embodies Plato's social ideal more fully than does the Ideal State. The Ideal State copes with the acceptance of luxuries by a sharp division between the property-sharing, familyless Guardians who lead a life of duty and service, and the property-owning Third Class who are totally excluded from political power. Between the writing of the *Republic* and the writing of the *Laws*, Plato's understanding of human psychology has undergone significant development as instanced in, for example, the recognition in the *Philebus* of the importance of pleasure in human life. This has led in turn to a change in Plato's attitude to property ownership and the acquisition of wealth. Greed and

avarice are still evils to be avoided or restrained, but the desire for
material goods and the enjoyment of them, the acceptance of
marriage and of family ties no longer mark a person out as
unsuited for political office.

Plato still argues for moderation: extremes of wealth and
poverty alike are to be avoided, but the design of Magnesia
demonstrates that he now accepts that successful landowning
farmers, conscientious family men, can attain the level of moral
and intellectual development that fits them for office as states-
men-lawgivers. Magnesia is not a reluctant compromise; it is not
a partial and inadequate realization of the ideal set out in the
Republic; it is the concrete manifestation of a new and different
ideal. Plato still believes philosophers should rule: he provides
that they should; he still believes a communism of wives and
property is an ideal, but he now believes it is possible to have a
state all of whose citizens own enough property to make their
households self-sufficient in basic necessities, who enjoy material
goods, who enjoy the pleasures of life in reasoned moderation,
who share in political responsibility, and who can throw up from
amongst their number men of sufficient virtue, wisdom, and
learning to exercise the office of statesman-lawgiver. That is new.
It is new and it is optimistic. The *Laws* may not be a masterpiece
of literary presentation, but it is a work of major philosophical
significance and of crucial importance to the understanding
of Plato's thought.

Magnesia, like the Ideal State of the *Republic*, is founded on
the principle of specialization. The citizen's main concern is the
life of virtue: civic duty, family responsibilities, religious observance, and military service provide the citizens with ample opportunity to exercise the virtues appropriate to their station. Ignoble
trades and crafts are left to foreigners and slaves. In charity to
him, we may reasonably speculate that, had Plato known that it
was possible to replace human labour with machines to perform
many of the dull and lowly tasks his model would leave to slaves,
then he might well have found no need to include the institution
of slavery in the economic and social structure of Magnesia.

Surprisingly, Plato follows the standard prejudice of Greek
political thinking in accepting a dual standard of rights and

duties, one for citizens another for resident non-citizens. I say surprisingly, since his own investigations of moral philosophy and of human psychology could reasonably be expected to have led him to design a society where the fullest opportunities for moral and intellectual development are open to all. In the end Plato remains an Athenian aristocrat: the farmer-soldiers of Magnesia are icons of an aristocratic ideal, even if an archaic aristocratic ideal. Plato's political philosophy remains coloured by a nostalgia for an imagined past.

If we emphasize the differential treatment of citizens and non-citizens, the *Laws* may be read as an elitist manifesto. Put back into its historical context it is nothing of the kind: given Plato's assumption that the state is for the citizens but will need the services of resident aliens and slaves to serve the citizens' needs, Magnesia becomes a remarkable vision of a balanced and ordered society, drawing together the openness of Athenian democracy and the stability and cohesiveness of Spartiate society under a system of laws designed to train the entire citizen body in personal, social, and civic virtue. That is not to say the design is flawless. The legal system involves such a degree of supervision of life it can easily be seen as unnecessarily and deadeningly restrictive. The censorship of art, while a recognition of the political significance of the arts in Plato's day, removes a source of creative influence. We should, perhaps, see Plato's harsh judgement on art as a judgement on the need to control communications and entertainment media rather than on a need to control the work of artists as such. In contemporary Athens the poet, the playwright, and the orator exercised an influence vastly greater than that exercised by artists in our own society. Even so, the degree of artistic censorship Plato proposes is disquietingly wide; we are surely justified in feeling that the rigid control of children's games is something of an extravagance.

The religious institutions of Magnesia are curious. Plato uses religion as a moral sanction: religious observance will bond the society together, and will cast an aura of sanctity over patterns of life which the law alone might not be able to enforce. The divine heavenly bodies are made objects of the cult in order to engender reverence for the providence of the souls which move and govern the Universe: oddly Plato now teaches there exists at least one Evil Soul which is responsible for the existence of evil and disorder in the world. It has been suggested that the Evil Soul could be a borrowing from Zoroastrianism: it well could, but it is not clear it is anything like an evil counterpart of the Cosmic Soul described in the *Timeaeus*.

The position of women in Magnesia deserves comment. In the *Republic* the women of the Guardian classes had equal rights and duties with the men. In Magnesia they share the same basic education and can hold certain offices in the state, but there is a much clearer differentiation of male and female roles. This is no doubt connected with the new importance given to marriage and family: Plato is operating with the Greek conception of the family as a patriarchal structure; women play a subordinate role in the family and hence are seen as playing a reduced role in the political and legal affairs of the society at large. We even find Plato putting into the mouth of the Athenian Stranger, who is his spokesman in the dialogue, conventional nonsense about the relative moral frailty of women. Even so the position of a married woman in Magnesia would be far preferable to that of her counterpart in Plato's Athens.

The *Laws* is Plato's last and his longest work. He writes under the shadow of approaching death to record his last vision of how a society can be designed which will provide for the material needs of all its citizens, offer them a pleasurable and enjoyable life, and at the same time school them in virtue. Plato himself thought this last intellectual enterprise worth the enormous effort it would cost a man of near eighty to write such a lengthy and complicated book. He left it in an imperfect state; but neglect of the *Laws* is unwise if we wish to understand Plato. For Plato, the philosopher finds his supreme fulfilment and his greatest enjoyment in the contemplation of ultimate reality, the supreme Forms and the transcendent principles they express, and in uncovering the complex network of relations amongst the Forms. His duty, however, is to put the knowledge he attains at the service of humanity: if the lot of human beings is to improve and their moral welfare to be promoted, their philosophers have a grave political duty. In the *Republic* Plato both diagnoses and fulfils this duty in laying down the blueprint for an Ideal State where philosophers rule a rationally organized society. The Ideal State of the *Republic* is an ideal, a pattern which can be used as a criterion to identify inadequacies in existing states. It lacks detail: it is inconceivable that it should ever exist as a political reality. Now at the end of his life Plato is compelled by his duty as a philosopher to create a new, fuller, and much more realistic design, a design which he is at last able to construct because of developments in his understanding of human psychology and of the significance of law, a design which is no longer an abstract ideal. Magnesia is a real possibility: no doubt details would need to be amended and improved, but in principle the colony could be established. Magnesia is not the perfect realization of Plato's social ideal, Plato himself acknowledges that: but it is so near to it that it has the constitutional, institutional, and cultural resources to produce its own philosopher-statesmen.

The *Laws* makes sense of Plato's philosophical activities in his later years. The abstract dialectical reasoning of the *Sophist* and the *Statesman*, the psychological analysis of the *Philebus*, the speculative cosmology of the *Timaeus* have been worthwhile philosophical enterprises on their own merits: the *Laws* demonstrates that they represent no flight from human concerns. Without the *Laws* Plato would be seen as retiring further and further into philosophical abstraction, having less and less involvement with the concrete problems of existence. The *Laws* demonstrates the reverse: his abstract technical philosophical studies have led to results which he now places at the service of humanity, designing a plan for the kind of society which could fulfil all the material, moral, and intellectual needs of mankind. Despite its inadequacies, the *Laws* is Plato's philosophical testament, and despite its inadequacies it is a work deserving serious attention. To ignore it is to turn a deaf ear to Plato's last words.

Further reading

If reading this book has kindled your interest in Plato and his thought, you may wish to find out more about the man and his philosophical work, and to explore different interpretations of his thought. Here are some suggestions as to books you would find interesting and useful.

General Works on Plato

Gosling, J.C.B., *Plato* (Routledge & Keegan Paul, 'Arguments of the Philosophers' series, London, 1973).

Hall, R.W., *Plato* (George Allen & Unwin, 'Political Thinkers' series, ed. Geraint Parry, London, 1981).

Hare, R.M., *Plato* (Oxford, 1982).

White, N.P., *Plato On Knowledge And Reality* (Hackett, Indianapolis, 1976).

These four modern works are all eminently readable and will provide a useful introduction to recent approaches to Plato. Amongst the many older works on Plato, the following may be found of particular interest:

Taylor, A.E., *Plato, The Man And His Work* (London, 1926). (This, despite its dated and implausible approach to the Socratic problem, is a classic study of Plato. It contains a useful summary of Plato's dialogues and of the apochryphal works.)

Cornford, F.M., *Before and After Socrates* (London, 1932).

Grube, G.M.A., *Plato's Thought* (London, 1935).

Crombie, I.M., *Plato, The Midwife's Apprentice* (London, 1964).

—— *An Examination Of Plato's Doctrines* 2 vols. (London, 1962, 1963).

Works on the Republic

Readers will find the following three works a helpful introduction to the most widely studied Platonic text; Nicholas White's book contains a useful summary of the dialogue as well as a commentary.

Annas, J. *An Introduction to Plato's Republic* (Oxford, 1982).

Cross, R.C. and Woozley, A.D., *Plato's Republic: a Philosophical Commentary* (Macmillan, London, 1964).

White, N.P., *A Companion to Plato's Republic* (Blackwell, Oxford, 1979).

Other Works

Allen, R.E., *Plato's* Euthyphro *and the Earlier Theory of Forms* (New York, 1970).

—— ed., *Studies in Plato's Metaphysics* (London, 1965).

Cornford, F.M., *Plato's Theory of Knowledge* (London, 1935).

—— *Plato's Cosmology* (London, 1938). (A valuable introduction to and commentary on the *Timaeus*.)

—— *Plato and Parmenides* (London, 1939).

Findlay, J.N., *Plato, the Written and Unwritten Doctrines* (London, 1962).

Gulley, N., *Plato's Theory of Knowledge* (London, 1962).

—— *The Philosophy of Socrates* (London, 1968).

Guthrie, W.K.C., *A History of Greek Philosophy* vols. 4 and 5 (Cambridge, 1975, 1978).

Havelock, E.A., *Preface to Plato* (Oxford, 1963).

Irwin, T., *Plato's Moral Theory* (Oxford 1977).

Morrow, G.R., *Plato's Cretan City* (Princeton, 1960).

Popper, K.R., *The Open Society and its Enemies* vol. 1 (5th edn., London, 1966).

Raven, T.E., *Plato's Thought in the Making* (Cambridge, 1965).

Ritter, C., *The Essence of Plato's Philosophy* (London, 1933).

Robinson, R., *Plato's Earlier Dialectic* (2nd edn., Oxford, 1953).

Ross, W.D., *Plato's Theory of Forms* (Oxford, 1953).

Runciman, W.G., *Plato's Later Epistemology* (Cambridge, 1962).

Sprague, R.K., *Plato's Use of Fallacy* (London, 1962).

Stalley, R.F., *Introduction to Plato's* Laws (Oxford, 1983).

Vlastos, G., *Platonic Studies* (Princeton, 1973).

—— ed., *Plato* 2 vols. (New York, 1971).

White, N.P., *Plato on Knowledge and Reality* (Indianapolis, 1976).

Index

OXFORD

MORE OXFORD PAPERBACKS

Details of a selection of other books follow. A complete list of Oxford Paperbacks, including The World's Classics, Twentieth-Century Classics, OPUS, Past Masters, Oxford Authors, Oxford Shakespeare, and Oxford Paperback Reference, is available in the UK from the General Publicity Department, Oxford University Press (JN), Walton Street, Oxford OX2 6DP.

In the USA, complete lists are available from the Paperbacks Marketing Manager, Oxford University Press, 200 Madison Avenue, New York, NY 10016.

Oxford Paperbacks are available from all good bookshops. In case of difficulty, customers in the UK can order direct from Oxford University Press Bookshop, 116 High Street, Oxford, Freepost, OX1 4BR, enclosing full payment. Please add 10 per cent of published price for postage and packing.

PHILOSOPHICAL EXPLANATIONS

Robert Nozick

In this highly original work, Robert Nozick develops new views on philosophy's central topics and weaves them into a unified philosophical perspective. It is many years since a major work in English has ranged so widely over philosophy's fundamental concerns: the identity of the self, knowledge and scepticism, free will, the question of why there is something rather than nothing, the foundations of ethics, the meaning of life.

Writing in a distinctive and personal philosophical voice, Professor Nozick presents a new mode of philosophizing. In place of the usual semi-coercive philosophical goals of proof, of forcing people to accept conclusions, this book seeks philosophical explanations and understanding, and thereby stays truer to the original motivations for being interested in philosophy.

'Philosophical discussion is bound to be influenced by its rich resources of fresh techniques and possibilities.' *Times Higher Educational Supplement*

PLATO

R. M. Hare

Even after twenty-three centuries, Plato's work remains the starting-point for the study of logic, metaphysics, and moral and political philosophy. But though his dialogues retain their freshness and immediacy, they can be difficult to follow. R. M. Hare has provided a short introduction to Plato's work that makes their meaning clear.

'in less then ninety pages [R. M. Hare] makes [this] monumental subject real, intelligible, and interesting' *Times Literary Supplement*

Past Masters

THREE ESSAYS

John Stuart Mill

On Liberty
Representative Government
The Subjection of Women

With an introduction by Richard Wollheim

The three major essays collected in this volume, written in the latter half of the life of John Stuart Mill (1806–73), were quickly accepted into the canon of European political and social thought. Nothing that has occurred in the intervening years has seriously affected their standing as classics on the subject. Today, although many of Mill's measures have been adopted, the essays are still relevant—when liberty and representative government are in collision with other principles, and when women still have to gain unprejudiced general acceptance of their equality.

In this introduction Richard Wollheim describes the essays as 'the distillation of the thinking of one highly intelligent, highly sensitive man, who spent the greater part of his life occupied with the theory and practice of society'.

ANCIENT GREEK LITERATURE

K. J. Dover

Sir Kenneth Dover and three classical scholars have collaborated in writing this new historical survey of Greek literature from 700 B.C. to 550 A.D. The book concentrates on the elements in Greek literature and attitudes to life which are unfamiliar to us, and to the elements which appear most powerfully to succeeding generations. Poetry, tragedy, comedy, history, science, and philosophy are all examined through the available literature.

MEN OF IDEAS

Some Creators of Contemporary Philosophy

Bryan Magee

In his successful BBC TV series 'Men of Ideas' Bryan Magee came face to face with fifteen of the world's foremost philosophers. The resulting discussions, edited transcripts of which appear in this book, add up to a lively yet authoritative introduction to much of the influential philosophy of our time.

'No clearer or more stimulating work on the creators of contemporary philosophy has appeared since Bertrand Russell's *History of Western Philosophy.*' *Books and Bookmen*

THE PROBLEMS OF PHILOSOPHY

Bertrand Russell

First published in 1912, this classic introduction to the subject of philosophical inquiry has proved invaluable to the formal student and general reader alike. It has Russell's views succinctly stated on material reality and idealism, knowledge by acquaintance and by description, induction, knowledge of general principles and of universals, intuitive knowledge, truth and falsehood, the distinctions between knowledge, error, and probable opinion, and the limits and the value of philosophical knowledge.

A foreword Russell wrote in 1924 for a German translation has been added as an appendix. Here Russell gave details of how some of his views had changed since *The Problems of Philosophy* was written.

An OPUS book

FREE WILL AND RESPONSIBILITY

Jennifer Trusted

'Jennifer Trusted's aim in *Free Will and Responsibility* is to introduce the stubborn problem of free will to beginners in philosophy and at the same time to make some contribution of her own to its solution. She writes lucidly, displays a wide acquaintance with the relevant literature, from Aristotle onwards, and packs a great deal of argument and exposition into a relatively small compass.' A. J. Ayer, *New Humanist*

'a determined, methodical onslaught on one of the classical, most familiar problems—or entanglement of problems—of philosophy since its earliest days . . . the well-trodden ground is clearly and sensibly traced out, and the readers for whom it is intended should indeed be helped by it—which is no mean achievement.' G. J. Warnock, *Expository Times*

MORAL PHILOSOPHY

D. D. Raphael

Do moral philosophers have anything to say which is useful, let alone comprehensible, to people with more down-to-earth concerns? Professor Raphael would answer 'Yes' on both counts. Unlike most 'introductions' to moral philosophy, this book is written expressly for the beginner. Also, it is not confined to the theory of ethics in any narrow sense, but makes a point of showing the connections between abstract ethics and practical problems.

'It would be difficult to find a clearer introduction to modern moral philosophy.' *Tablet*

An OPUS book

THE LEGACY OF GREECE

A New Appraisal

Edited by M. I. Finley

This book is about much more than 'the glory that was Greece'. Each of the fourteen distinguished contributors describes a particular aspect of Greek culture, and then shows what later generations have made of this valuable inheritance. The result is a lucid and down-to-earth introduction to how the ancient Greeks lived and thought, and to their influence on the world today. Topics covered include politics, literature, history, education, philosophy, science, myth, and art and architecture.

'An important and fascinating book [which] provides a fundamental explanation of the significance of Greece to Western European civilization. It should be read by all concerned in understanding this.' *British Book News*

THE GREAT PHILOSOPHERS

From Plato to the Present Day

Bryan Magee

Beginning with the death of Socrates in 399, and following the story through the centuries to recent figures such as Bertrand Russell and Wittgenstein, Bryan Magee and fifteen contemporary writers and philosophers provide an accessible and exciting introduction to Western philosophy and its greatest thinkers.

'Magee is to be congratulated . . . anyone who sees the programmes or reads the book will be left in no danger of believing philosophical thinking is unpractical and uninteresting.' Ronald Hayman, *Times Educational Supplement*

'one of the liveliest, fast-paced introductions to philosophy, ancient and modern, that one could wish for' *Universe*